WINDOWS OF *Wonder*
DISCOVERING EXTRAORDINARY W.O.W.
MOMENTS IN THE ORDINARY

LISA WILT

To Daniela

Live wonder
filled!

RX FOR THE SOULFUL HEART

~

Windows Of Wonder: Discovering Extraordinary W.O.W. Moment in the Ordinary Moments.

Cover Photo-Anderson Photography

~

~

This book is dedicated to my Dad and Mom
–Cliff and Rose Nale–
whose last name is pronounced like the word nail.
Truly they nailed it loving Kathy, Brian and me unconditionally.
By their example I learned the value of Godly wisdom
coupled with a hard day's work.
Who could ask for better?

~

In loving memory of my friend Laura Stagg,
who no longer has to look through the
window and wonder what heaven will be like.

~

For now we see through a glass, darkly;
but then face to face: now I know in part;
but then shall I know even as also I am known.
**1 Corinthians 13:12

"Lisa's servant's heart shines in *Windows of Wonder*. She takes you on a Daily Faith Journey that reminds you there are so many wonderful moments in our lives to be WOWED by!"

—Gail Carlock President and CEO Heartwork Inspires and a Zig Ziglar Certified Speaker

"Few, very few feelings of true wonder do we actually acknowledge as moments of wonder and rejoice about them. Lisa Wilt has written a fabulous book reminding us that wonder is all around us in our daily lives. Those that see all the wonder, know it comes from the hand of God. This book will remind you daily of how blessed we are to be children of a God that can save us, teach us and show us moments of wonder when we least expect it. A terrific read for anyone wanting to feel the real meaning of life."

–Jerry Acuff President and CEO of Delta Point and Best Selling Author of The Relationship Edge.

DANDY LION ACKNOWLEDGMENTS

*A*t three, my precious Alyssa would burst through the backdoor with her two hands cupped in excitement as she held golden treasures. Hidden in her hands she had the yellow flower tops she had plucked from dandelions leaving the stems behind.

"I brought you the good parts, Momma," she would share in excitement, "Lots of them!" I would applaud her achievement. Then together we would fill an *ordinary* bowl with water and transform it into an *extra-ordinary* swimming pool centerpiece for "the lions that are dandy," as she used to call them.

While some people may think of "Dandy Lions" as *ordinary* weeds, we saw their floating flower faces and thought they were *extra-ordinary.*

*Reverend Mike Costanzo–You looked at my dandelion

devotions and saw "the good parts" insuring theological accuracy. Thank you for your *extra-ordinary* expertise and wisdom.

*Jonna Beenken, Sharon Baker and Rachel Smith–Thank you for helping make my stemless dandelions' faces seamless, wonder-filled treasures.

*My Heavenly Father–You deserve so much more than this weedy bouquet of dandy lion devotions. Thank you for sharing **W.O.W.** moments when I slowed down enough to peek through Your **Window of Wonder**. You alone can satiate my **hunger for wonder**.

Someday I'll join You at Your banquet table.
I **wonder** what type of centerpieces you'll have?

Alyssa–now 25–and me holding a swimming pool centerpiece of "Lions that are Dandy."

A huge THANK YOU to my W.O.W. Launch Team: Dawn Anderson, Lynn Arnold, Chris Blackburn, Judy Chandler, Lesli Cutshall, Traci Dryer, Jennifer Eberhardt, Phyllis Elliott, Amanda Enloe, Cheryl Eustis, Alyssa Falck, Debby Falck, Amanda Hanna, Elaine Hanshaw, Carol Hjort, Rachel Jensen, Georgia Johnson, Donna Kilgore, Ronni Lickert, Christa Lane, Ceil Lynch, Missy Marcella, Michelle Matherly, Kelly Ogle, Luisa Pattison, Cyndi Scarlett, Kim Shelton, Roxanne Smith, Shelly Trear and Angie Williams.

INTRODUCTION

MY HUNGER FOR WONDER

$\mathcal{M}$y kitchen window needs washing. My routine life needs **wonder**!

Beyond my sink window splattered with dirty dishwater stood a Momma doe watching her two bouncing baby fawns. Like my two children, they were full of **wonder** and excitement. They scampered in circles around her as she stood dutifully guarding her little ones. Unlike her kiddos, she didn't expend the energy to frolic.

As I stood scrubbing the spaghetti sauce pan, I wondered if she, like me, was weary. I felt connected to this momma deer. I sensed she knew I was watching her as she watched her fawns. Lowering her head to take a bite, she nibbled at the sweet clover, a treat my husband had planted specifically for wildlife. I was glad she had a moment to enjoy something better than ordinary grass.

I wondered if she rarely had moments when she could stop and savor life. I wondered what she thought as she saw her little ones' scamper through the clover so happy.

I wondered how long it had been since she had skipped merrily. I wondered when she, like me, stopped leaping and started being so stoic and so grown up.

The microwave beeped interrupting our solitude. I was warming water for tea, a treat for me when I finished cleaning the kitchen. Gazing out the window with my mug cupped in my hands—now free from rubber gloves—I wondered, why aren't I more like those fawns bouncing in a field of wide open **wonder**.

Such simple beauty can inspire and impart strength. In the depth of that moment, I was energized and encouraged. I had such clarity of vision and such peace.

An *ordinary* day of chores became *extraordinary* in those moments. That was a **WOW** moment–a **Window of Wonder** moment! Thus, was born the idea for Windows of Wonder (W.O.W.).

I **hunger for wonder**. Do you?

Between the ordinary slices of my life as a working wife, a mom and a pharmacist, does God sandwich meaty glimpses of His glory? While there are still mounds of meals to be made and loads of clothes to be laundered, does He hide **W.O.W.** moments between dirty dishes and dirty socks?

Even though my kitchen window is clouded, can He sharpen my spiritual vision so that it is Windex® clear as I look for the unexpected in the expected routine of my days? Will you walk with me on a spiritual journey looking for **wonder**, not just in the pages of this book but in the story of your life?

Honestly, my husband—an outdoorsman—has always been more of a nature watcher than me. I watch for sales and coupons. But maybe I can learn from Him how to slow down and appreciate glimpses of God's glory in nature and in family. Maybe God will speak to me through my work as a pharmacist.

Since my most cherished job is being a mom, I pray He will provide **W.O.W.** moments in my upside-down desperate moments of motherhood. After all, **W.O.W.** when turned upside down does spell "M.O.M.," right?

Let's take this journey together searching for **wonder**!

Let's ask God to be our guide. And let's turn to His Word for inspiration. Though our eyes may still have raccoon remnants of mascara when we peer in the mirror each morning, let's search for the majestic in the mundane.

Even if we have to race to roll the garbage cans to the curb in our robes on trash day, can we be still enough to hear Him speak in the daily pace that numbs us to **wonder**?

Breathe deep and exhale purposefully with me. It's a Mount Rushmore-sized challenge to rush less. Will you take the journey with me?

Together let's **hunger for wonder**!

Grab your fork and reading glasses. Let's feast on each day's delectable moments making everyday a holiday. Let's giggle, sigh, weep, and smile...but most of all, let's bask in the light of His magnificence.

He who created the sun, the moon and the starfish wants you and me to slow down, relax and experience **Windows of Wonder**. Let's be **wowed** together.

THROUGH A WINDOW

One of my Dad's favorite stories to tell is one about my brother–Brian–who at the time was all of four and filled with **wonder**. We called him Barney Blue Bell, which is a whole "nother" story in itself.

Like most boys his age, he was in perpetual motion. There was a lot to do...to discover...to dismantle...to destroy and the backyard was an open abyss of adventure and **wonder**.

Our screen door never latched, which wasn't a problem because no one in the quiet town of Mattoon, Illinois ever locked their doors. In the summer Brian would race toward the door, slam the Plexiglas® with both hands shoving the door open, and be on his way sailing down the steps.

There was one day, however, that was different. Unbeknown to him, Dad had taken the Plexiglas out to replace it, as it was marred making it was far from transparent. You can guess what happened. Brian literally sailed through the opening and somersaulted down the steps.

Alarmed, my father raced to his aid. But like most little BIG boys, he was a tough tyke. Barney dusted off his britches glancing back at the door in amazed confusion. Then He looked up at my Dad and squinted, wrinkling his little nose he asked, "Where's the window?"

DO YOU EVER EXPERIENCE DAYS WHERE YOU ARE RUNNING FULL speed toward a goal and suddenly find yourself figuratively somersaulting unexpectedly down a set of stairs? I had one of those days recently and I thought of this story my dad loves to tell.

The innocence of Barney's question has always brought a smile to my face, but today it also ushered in a **W.O.W.** moment. Now decades later, my Dad has Parkinson's Disease and he is looking through a whole "nother" window. A window that separates Earth from eternity.

My Dad cherishes verses like those found in **1 Corinthians 13:12, where Saint Paul looks forward to heaven as he explains:

"For now, we see through a glass, darkly;
but then face to face:
now I know in part;
but then shall I know even as also I am known."

When we read descriptions of heaven in the Bible, it is much like looking through a scratched Plexiglas window that is clouded with life's abrasions and fingerprints. We struggle to see from this side of eternity, the perfectness of what is to come?

The Bible shares some **W.O.W.** glimpses into the eternal. In Saint John's preview of heaven in Revelation 21:4 we learn that God will wipe every tear from our eyes, and there will be no more death or sorrow or crying or pain. All these things will be gone forever.

I look forward to that day. For now, every day on this earth is smudged with some imperfection but every tear cried today can serve as a rainbow promise of sorts reminding us of the day there will be no more tears.

Years ago, when I went to pharmacy school my mom returned to college to become a nurse. She found her place in hospice care, loving her patients as they stepped through the back door into eternity.

Perhaps this is why I find a book written by a hospice nurse so meaningful. My mom, like Trudy Harris the author of *Glimpses of Heaven: True Stories of Hope and Peace at the End of Life's Journey*, saw glimpses into heaven through the eyes of her patients.

During Trudy's four decades as a hospice nurse, she sat with her patients as they faced death reassuring them that they were not alone and that they were loved. Trudy's patients came from all backgrounds and all walks of life. Some were children, others middle-aged and still others fragile from the years, yet their experiences share a few common threads.

Those who are dying can see those they love, as if they are looking through a window. They are comforted by them and feel their presence like a warm blanket fresh from the dryer on a chilly morning.

There is a peace that permeates their spirit like sunlight streaming through a window brightens a shadowed room. This sunlight dispels fear.

Early in her career, Trudy dismissed what her patients saw, felt, heard and even smelled to hallucinations caused by the medications. But when similar experiences were shared by patients who were not medicated, Trudy began to listen more attentively.

Universally, those who were dying spoke of a love so powerful and so inviting, their souls longed to be completely enveloped and present in heaven. Many heard choral melodies serenaded by angels that soothed their sleep. Others smelled bouquets of sweet fragrances.

All these descriptions align with what we learn from God's Word about heaven, many of these descriptions reiterated again and again (Job 38:7, Psalms 148:2, Song of Songs 4:10-14, Ezekiel 1:26, Hosea 14:6, Revelation 4:3, Revelation 5:8-11, Revelation 7:11, Revelation 10:1, Revelation 15:6). I believe God shares these images so that we can fearlessly look forward to being welcomed home.

For this reason I am not surprised to read that Trudy's near-death patients explain that the colors they see when peering into heaven are even more exquisitely vibrant than anything they have ever experienced.

Here on earth, scientists estimate that our human eye can detect about 10,000,000 different colors. I am blown away by God's attention to detail in His design of us, this world and heaven.

I can hardly fathom 10,000,000 different colors here nor can I–a person who loves adjectives–imagine the creative work of naming 10,000,000 plus colors. But I love to envision it!

As a child, I fondly remember my concept of heaven's perfection in the coveted large bonus box of Crayolas® with the sharpener built in. To have all new crayons with perfect points at the start of the school year seemed to be a sliver of the heavenly perfection to come. But Crayolas never stayed nice for long.

After the first week, only colors like Bittersweet and Raw Sienna still had perfect points. Even at five, I didn't want my family of stick people to live in the bittersweet world of raw sienna.

In heaven I am convinced based on God's Word that nothing will taste bittersweet and no hurts will be raw (Romans 8:18). Maybe it's the pharmacist in me, but I especially appreciate knowing that in heaven there will be Trees of Life with leaves that will provide medicine for the healing of all nations and peoples (Revelation 22:2).

An even more brilliant **W.O.W.** moment is found in verses 3-4a:

"No longer will there be a curse upon anything.
For the throne of God and of the Lamb will be there,

and his servants will worship him.
And they will see his face."

How do you imagine God's face...is He smiling? In your mind's eye, how do you envision the eyes of Jesus?

Someday we will no longer have to wonder what artist on earth has best captured the kindness in His eyes because the window that separates us from eternity with Him will be removed...just like my Father removed the Plexiglas window from our back door.

All our questions, much like my little brother's, will be answered.

THE JOURNEY FORWARD:

I have lots of dirty windows in my house that I can't see through perfectly. Do you have one window or mirror that needs cleaned?

If so, can you find your Windex and paper towels and as you clean, anticipate the promise of John 14:2:

"There is plenty of room for you in my Father's home.
If that weren't so, would I have told you that
I'm on my way to get a room ready for you?"

My prayer is that knowing this can help you. It helps me journey through the less than perfect days. And it allows me to find joy in the fact that through Jesus, you and I are destined for a happily ever after. Together we can rest in His assurance and give Him our fears.

P.B.J. HOR D'OEUVRES

WITH COLORED TOOTHPICKS

*M*y Mom was always very health conscious. She was a lot of fun too. So, when the little girls in my neighborhood would be over pretending in my playhouse, Mom would bring out hors d'oeuvres with colored toothpicks in each one.

She made the best snacks on the block...double-decker peanut butter and strawberry jelly sandwiches, cut into sixteenths, with an extra layer of peanut butter on top. She liked us to have the extra protein.

Over twenty years later, I still smile when I eat P.B.J.'s, which is why I choose PBJ hors d'oeuvres to be our reminder today to always **hunger for wonder.**

I remember so wanting to be like her, to be a mom and to wear lipstick. When my brother, sister, and I would walk to

Eisner's grocery store to pick out candy, I would always pick the sweet tart lipstick dispenser candy.

When the candy was gone, Mom would replace the lipstick with a baby carrot stick. What fond memories do you have from childhood?

Most every day we walked home from St. Mary's School eight blocks west on Richmond Avenue across the viaduct. Mom would greet us at the door frequently with hot oatmeal raisin cookies. Sometimes she made chocolate chip cookies, but she would always slip some raisins in them too.

"Raisins are good for you," she would remind us.

At the time, we didn't appreciate her efforts. I loved to go to Kelly Barton's house down on Annis Avenue because she had Chips Ahoy cookies that came in a blue bag. It was a big deal to have cookies from the store. I just got homemade. Isn't it funny how our perspective changes with age?

As WE HUNGER FOR WONDER, LET'S LOOK FOR THE EXTRA-ordinary in the ordinary. A PBJ sandwich may be *ordinary*, but my mom made it *extraordinary*. Do you have any foods that you make extra special with love?

If you care for children, you probably spend a chunk of time each week buying and preparing food then cleaning up after meals. Even eating out takes time. How much time would you estimate you spend on food? While good nutrition is para-mount, as we **hunger for wonder** I ask myself, am I more concerned with my family's physical diet than with our spiritual diet?

Do I spend more time on physically feeding my family's bodies than spiritually feeding their souls? Food is important, but Christ points out that people cannot thrive just eating bread.

We need to hear God—His Word feeds our spirit. Likewise, Moses stresses the need for God's Words telling us to write His commands on our hearts in Deuteronomy 6:6-7:

"Get them inside of you and then get them inside your children.
Talk about them wherever you are,
sitting at home or walking in the street;
talk about them from the time you get up in the morning
to when you fall into bed at night."

Wow. That's a lot of time. So basically, this verse is telling me to internalize God's Word, to consume His Words like I would eat good food. And to share God's Word, like I would share good food…wherever I go.

These verses are part of the "Shema." It is one of only two prayers that are specifically commanded in the Torah—the first five books of the Bible. These are foundational to both the Jewish and the Christian faith.

It is part of the oldest daily prayer in Judaism and has been recited morning and night since ancient times. While we may not recite the Shema to begin and end each day, we too want to consistently nourish our children with God's Word.

I have found that having a Christian radio station playing in my car and home has been a wonderful way to saturate my children with God's love and His Word every day of the week.

Bedtime stories also make a great time for Bible stories. After all, these are the biographies of our Patriarchs and heroes of the faith rather than the fictional fairytales that Disney creates, though these are fun too.

One of the traditions that my mother began nearly three decades ago, was blessing each my sister, my brother and myself when we woke up and then again before bedtime. She physically made the sign of the cross on our foreheads with her thumb and reminded us:

"You are a child of God,
taught of the Lord,
great will be your peace and undisturbed composure."

She gleaned this promise from Psalm 54:13 and must have had an Amplified Bible, Classic Edition at the time because this is the only translation that uses the unique phrase "undisturbed composure."

Of all the blessings she could have chosen to pray over me, this verse translated in this way has done more to empower and change my life than any other. It has been perfectly tailored for me.

Both my Creator and my mother know my weaknesses (I have many). They knew I would need this verse to make it through the rigors of Pharmacy School.

They knew I would need this promise as the helpmate of a

much-stressed physician, who works eighty hour weeks. And they knew I would need this truth as a mother, who has type A tendencies and is wired to worry. I have started this tradition of blessing my own children and those senior high youth at my church who are entrusted to my care.

Yes. We are rightfully concerned about the physical body that we can see. But how much more important is the unseen? Do we spend an equal amount of time, or even one third of the time, tending to spiritual food?

Our physical bodies will pass away, but our spirits and souls can live eternally with our Creator, which is why I choose food today as we **hunger for wonder**.

THE JOURNEY FORWARD:

Do you keep a Bible in the kitchen so that you can snack on His Word? I have personally found a nibble here and there really adds up. So when you're waiting on your morning coffee to brew, have a bite of The Bread of Life found in His Word.

Are you hungry now? Maybe you could make yourself a PBJ sandwich cut into hors d'oeuvre size bites or if you're not hungry have a sample a Scripture hors d' oeuvre from John 6:35a:

"I am the bread of life.
Whoever comes to me will never be hungry again."

THROUGH THE WINDSHIELD

*A*s you're driving on a scorching summer day, have you ever seen what appears to be water on the highway's horizon? It's an elusive puddle covering the pavement. Like me, have you have come to recognize this is a mirage and mentally dismiss it?

What we are seeing are heat waves rising up from the road. The waves deceivingly appear to be water. The placement of the puddle is dependent upon the angle of reflection of the waves off the earth's surface. As you move closer, the water seemingly moves farther from you. Try as you might, you never reach the illusion.

A MIRAGE CAN BE A **WINDOW OF WONDER** MOMENT, PROVIDING A

perspective-changing lesson on joy. Just as we never experience driving through the puddle of water, some never experience lasting joy in their lives. To them, joy is distant and elusive like a mirage. Perhaps it is because they expect to be joyful

when they reach the horizon...

when they are finally able to slow down...

when they have time for themselves...

when their kids are grown...

when they are not trapped by an embankment of bills...

when they can finally take that vacation...

when their health improves.

Does someone specific come to mind when you hear this list? If I'm honest, sometimes I find myself thinking, that I would be more joyful if only...

my husband was kinder...

my kids were more obedient...

my boss was fairer...

my hair was thicker.

And the list goes on.

Do you too find yourself making those "if only" statements too? What do your joyless days look and feel like? Honestly, I'm weak when I am weary and joyless. Those days I seem to misplace joy just as I misplace my cell phone, my husband misplaces his T.V. remote and my daughter misplaces her blankie. Yet even when I feel devoid of joy, I am not alone.

When I am having a particularly joyless day, I remind myself that I can turn to God and experience His joy through His Spirit. You can too as Galatians 5:22 assures us:

"The Holy Spirit produces this kind of fruit in our lives:
love, **joy**, peace, patience, kindness, goodness,
faithfulness, gentleness, and self-control."

I find it telling that joy is recorded second only to love in the list of nine fruit of the Spirit. Could this indicate that joy is important? I definitely think so. In fact, I think joy is as essential to our spirits as water is to our bodies. As humans, water is second only to oxygen in the hierarchy of our physical needs. We can survive about five minutes without air and five days without water.

Joy hydrates and satiates our souls. Joy is real, not some puddle on the pavement that is never quite within our reach based on the truth of *1 John 1:3-4:

"Now we're telling you so you can experience it along with us,
this experience of communion with the Father and his Son,
Jesus Christ. Our motive for writing is simply this:
We want you to enjoy this, too.
Your joy will double our joy!"

Like St John, that's my prayer for our journey…that together we will have double our joy through communion with God, Who wants to drench us with joy.

Do you thirst for joy as you **hunger for wonder**? I am encouraged, and in a sense hydrated, when I hear about others in the Bible who faced worse trials than mine.

We can read about the apostles who were under incredible

stress, facing inconceivable odds. While they had Good News, not everyone thought it was good. The Jewish religious leaders believed the Good News was blasphemy while the Roman leaders thought it would usher in anarchy.

In *2 Corinthians 6:1-10 Paul honestly shares his trials knowing that people like us can be encouraged when we see how they faced difficulties:

"in hard times, tough times, bad times; when we're beaten up,
jailed, and mobbed; working hard,
working late, working without eating; with pure heart, clear
head, steady hand; in gentleness, holiness, and honest love;
when we're telling the truth,
and when God's showing his power;
when we're doing our best setting things right;
when we're praised, and when we're blamed; slandered, and
honored; true to our word, though distrusted;
ignored by the world, but recognized by God;
terrifically alive, though rumored to be dead;
beaten within an inch of our lives, but refusing to die;
immersed in tears, yet always filled with deep joy."

I counted sixteen negative experiences yet each are counter balanced with a positive and Paul shares that they were "always filled with deep joy." Can we say the same when life is rough? Even my very worst days are not as bad as those experienced by Paul.

Saint Peter also knows what rough days feel like and encourages us in 1 Peter 1:6 to:

"Be truly glad! There is wonderful joy ahead,
even though the going is rough for a while down here."

Then he describes our faith as Christians in the twenty-first century and gives us another reason to be filled with joy in verse 8a:

"You love him even though you have never seen him;
though not seeing him, you trust him;
and even now you are happy with the inexpressible joy
that comes from heaven itself."

We are given a shout out and praised for our faith because we believe even though we have not physically seen Jesus. Someday we will see Jesus and while there will be perfect joy in heaven, even now in imperfect circumstances, we can experience "inexpressible joy."

So, when joy feels impossible to reach like that mirage, know that what Saint Paul wrote and prayed in Romans 15:13 is meant for us too:

"I pray that God, the source of hope,
will fill you completely with joy and peace
because you trust in him.
Then you will overflow with confident hope

through the power of the Holy Spirit."

This passage tells me that God is the source or Wellspring of hope. Do you thirst for joy as you **hunger for wonder**? It's something others want...that others need. Our joy draws others who are thirsty to the Wellspring.

Jesus understands that work can be scorching, kids can be draining, and that relationships have dry spells. And that's exactly when you and I need His joy most. When it is sweltering outside the natural phenomena of heat waves appear to remind us that—unlike mirages—His joy is real!

THE JOURNEY FORWARD:

Jesus understands that work can be scorching, kids can be draining, and that relationships have dry spells. And that's exactly when you and I need His joy most. When it is sweltering outside the natural phenomena of heat waves appear to remind us that—unlike mirages—His joy is real!

Until then, can you look out a window and see a horizon? Even though you can't see what lies beyond the horizon, you know that it is as real as what is right outside your window.

Likewise, joy is real and within your reach!

DOUGHNUTS WITH SPRINKLES

At the end of the frozen-food aisle
is the bakery,
and at the bakery
there are doughnuts,
and the doughnuts have sprinkles.
Lots and lots of colorful sprinkles!

The more sprinkles,
"the more yummier,"
a little girl explains to her momma
before she presses her tiny hands and pudgy nose
against the glass to admire
the kaleidoscope of colors.

For the first time
since she bounced across
the threshold of the supermarket,
she is still.
In silence,
she admires the doughnuts.

The clerk notices her.
He asks if she needs assistance.
She doesn't know the word "assistance",
but she knows she wants that doughnut.
Eyes pleading with anticipation,
she turns toward her mother.

Will they leave without the doughnut,
or will they merely leave
the finger and nose prints on the glass
from a little girl
who peered through the **window with wonder**
at the doughnut with sprinkles?

*a*s we walk toward the check-out, Alyssa merrily skips in front of our cart swinging her cellophane bakery bag which contains—yes you guessed it—the doughnut with sprinkles.

Seeing her skip inspires me to skip too. Almost three, my daughter's **hunger for wonder** is satisfied with sprinkles. I wonder what she will hunger when she is twenty-three…thirty-three…even forty-three?

FOR WHAT DO YOU HUNGER TODAY? THOUGH FEW OF US GAZE with **wonder** through a bakery window at the colorful sprinkles on a doughnut, I spend time gazing through the window to the world provided by my computer and television. I sometimes gaze at the beautiful models who are promoting skin-care products and long for a perfect complexion. Do you?

We gaze through the windows of department stores. Sometimes we gaze through the windows of prospective homes on the market. We gaze in showrooms with new cars. Then we gaze through the windows at the immaculate interiors of the shiny cars (with no sprinkles from doughnuts scattered on the upholstery).

You and I can gaze at the exciting lives of others on Facebook and long for more excitement in our own lives. Perhaps we gaze at the exciting vacation locations and long for the finances to fund such fun.

But I ask myself, will these truly satisfy, or will they leave me with even more hunger? Are the desires that the marketing executives would want for you and me the desires that God would want for us? Are the world's desires, God's desires? Most importantly, are our desires, God's desires? We are told in Psalm 37:3-5:

"Trust in the Lord and do good.
Then you will live safely in the land and prosper.
Take delight in the Lord,
and he will give you your heart's desires.
Commit everything you do to the Lord.
Trust him, and he will help you."

Often just the bolded promise is plucked and quoted out of context, like my daughter plucks the pink sprinkles from her doughnut. This passage is misunderstood when people use it to petition the Lord for desirable, tangible items. Above the word "desire" refers to a craving. Asking the Lord to provide the desires of our heart is asking that He provide our hungers.

The first half of the conditional promise tell us to "Trust in the Lord and do good." Then we are told to "Take delight in the Lord." I love the verbs "trust" and "delight." We could all use more trust and delight, wouldn't you agree?

Sometimes our responsibilities are so heavy, that it's hard to trust and be light hearted, delighting in God and His small blessings...like sprinkles on a doughnut. I could learn a lot from my children about both trusting and delighting.

THE JOURNEY FORWARD:

Do you have a container of colorful sprinkles in your spice cabinet? If so, could you put them on your countertop this week as a reminder to search for **wonder** in the small, colorful experiences that God sprinkles throughout your mundane moments?

If you don't have sprinkles why not put them on your grocery list? Ask the Lord to give you the desires He would want you to have and read the remainder of Psalm 37. He wants your life to be sprinkled with satisfying **wonder**!

PERSPIRATION

*W*hat is lifeless and ice cold but sweats? It can also provide us with a **W.O.W.** observation. Need a hint? If you have a cold drink in your hand, the answer may be at your fingertips; it is inanimate or lifeless, and it "sweats." Have you ever wondered how this happens?

Warm air holds more water than cold air. Think of how dry air is during winter and how humid air is in the tropics. When the warmer air outside the glass comes in contact with the surface, its molecules slow down becoming closer together. They condense. Condensation is the name of the wonderful process of gaseous vapor turning back into liquid water droplets.

Evaporation is the exact opposite of condensation. For evaporation to occur, the liquid molecules gain energy, usually through heat, becoming excited and bouncing around, moving farther and farther apart until they become a vapor. This is seen when water boils in a pan. Energy or heat is lost in the process.

God gave us sweat glands so that when sweat evaporates, we lose energy or heat, just like the pan of boiling water. It's His way of cooling us down.

We call this perspiration. In our **hunger for wonder**, we are learning all sorts of fun facts without working up a sweat.

WHILE PERSPIRING CONTROLS OUR EXCESS BODY HEAT, GOD ALSO provides a way for us to stay emotionally cool and controlled. A few pages ago, we read about joy in **Galatians 5:22-23 and learned that in Christ we have all nine fruit of the Spirit. This time, focus particularly on the last one listed:

> "The fruit of the Spirit is love, joy, peace, longsuffering,
> gentleness, goodness, faith, meekness, **temperance**:
> against such there is no law."

While many newer translations of God's Word replace *temperance* with *self-control*, I like the old English word of temperance for a few reasons. First, it takes "self" out of the equation. "Self" or the flesh is usually what has gotten me to the point that I am out of control.

When the first word out of my mouth is the word "I," that's a good indication to me that the conversation is self-centered rather than spirit-centered.

Some poor examples in my life that are the result of self-absorption begin with the statement "I don't know how much more I can take of your ____." or "I have had it with your continual _____." We all could fill in the blank differently.

There are thousands of self-help books on self-control in the self-improvement section of Barnes and Noble. When I am emotionally hot, what I need is less of myself and more of His Spirit.

Secondly, I like the word temperance because it is self-defining; it sounds like what it does. Merriam-Webster tells us that the word "temper" comes from the Latin word "temperāre" and means "to control." The suffix "ance" means "action or state."

Living in the Show Me State of Missouri, I like when the word shows me its meaning and makes sense. Controlling our temper or state is certainly a **W.O.W.** learning opportunity.

Anger is a hot subject.

When I'm mad, I personally need the Spirit to help me control my mouth. Now you may be wondering where you were when the Holy Spirit was granting temperance. You need not think you have missed a blessing.

You and I have all the self-control we will ever need. If you know Christ, you are filled with His Spirit and you have all nine of the Spirit's fruit. Granted, in me some may need to "ripen" a bit to be more palatable.

In order for our spiritual fruit to ripen, we can spend some time basking in the Light of His Son, reading His Word and talking to Him in prayer. I have found the Bible's books of wisdom a fantastic place to start reading.

In *Ecclesiastes 7:9 I learn a bit about anger and boomerangs:

> "Don't be quick to fly off the handle.
> Anger boomerangs.
> You can spot a fool by the lumps on his head."

Hmm...I've had a few boomerang bumps on my head. The lumps on my head have dropped me to my knees. From my knees, I can see things differently as I pray *Proverbs 19:11 which tells me:

> "Sensible people control their temper;
> they earn respect by overlooking wrongs."

I agree and I want to be known as sensible. While I have not arrived, I am still learning the truth of * Proverbs 15:1:

> "A gentle response defuses anger,
> but a sharp tongue kindles a temper-fire."

Oh, how I want my children to learn by my example how to neutralize the caustic acid of anger with basic gentleness. Dealing with angry people is a life skill, one that I use at work daily. It's a necessity for marriages that endure "for better or for worse." Gentle people make better friends, spouses and parents than those with angry, sharp tongues.

THE JOURNEY FORWARD:

Just as perspiring helps control our physical temperature, temperance helps control our emotional temper. So, the next time you perspire, thank God for His "Son Light" and for the spiritual gift of temperance.

On our journey today read Ephesians 4:26 below. Can you vow to live this truth and mentally fill in the missing vowels?

"Don't S _ N by letting anger control you.
Don't let the S _ N go down while you are still angry."

THE P.U.S. MAN

*I*f you are a parent, grandparent, aunt or uncle helping to raise children, have you found it to be the most rewarding and the most draining job ever? I'm inspired by mothers in the Bible like Hannah and Eunice. Even with their positive examples, some days seem to go from bad to worse like mud on little feet, that spreads to mud on the carpet, then to mud on the couch.

These are the rainy days as a M.O.M. when I'm turned upside down and desperately need a transforming **W.O.W.** moment. After all, MOM when turned upside-down does spell WOW!

At home during these times I will stop, often kneeling down, and pray with my daughter. Our prayer is simple. Usually we ask that I will be "more nicer," that Alyssa will be more obedient, and that baby Garrett will be less fussy.

I want my daughter to learn early in life that God can help us through the ordinary frustrations that keep us from experiencing His **wonder**. He encourages us to reach out to Him.

This morning after praying, I asked for Alyssa's forgiveness for my short-temper and explained that I just needed a few minutes of quiet time. In her attempt to be helpful she offered, "Momma, I go see Nana."

Great solution but a bit impractical since Grandma lived in central Illinois, over six hours from us in our Kansas City suburb. I smiled at the thought and chuckled, "Should I put a stamp on your forehead and stuff you in the mailbox?"

She wrinkled her little nose, cocked her sweet head and smiled. "I don't think you and baby Garrett would fit, do you?"

She giggled and spun around acting silly. Then she stopped mid-twirl with what she thought was a wonderful revelation, "Mom, the P.U.S. man can take me!" (She had her own **W.O.W.** moment.) Nearly every day, we receive packages from U.P.S. and if the boxes are big enough, once empty, she loves to play in them. A trip to Nana's in a box sounded like a brilliant idea to her.

She was ready to search for the packing tape. Now, she hopped up and down clapping. Her eager eyes twinkled in **wonder** and there it was: my simple **W.O.W.** moment.

Ahh...to see through the enthusiastic eyes of a toddler. Wouldn't it be nice if we could package up whatever frustrates us and mail it off? I could keep U.P.S. and Fed. Ex. really hopping. How about you?

Whether our trials are...

child-related,

spouse-related,

health-related,

job-related, or

money-related,

searching for God and the *extraordinary* in the *ordinary* is a spiritual discipline that helps. **Wonder** lightens our load, wouldn't you agree?

On an average day when you think of God, what images and adjectives first come to mind? So much of how we see God, and even this world, is shaped by experiences we had when we were young, the age of my children.

If you had wonderful loving parents, you may be more inclined to see God's **wonder** and experience His love.

If you had a difficult childhood with unreliable parents, you may see God as difficult and unreliable.

If you had parents who were easily angered, you may perceive God to be angry.

Today, as I sat down for my quiet time, it was not quiet in my house; I so **hungered for wonder**, I was a bit "hangry." This is what God spoke to me through the parchment thin pages of *Psalm 103:8-11:

"God is sheer mercy and grace;
not easily angered,

he's rich in love.
He doesn't endlessly nag and scold, nor hold grudges forever...
He knows us inside and out
and keeps in mind that we're made of mud."

I have to smile. How perfect for today—a day when I look and feel like mud and I have mud all over the family room—to be reminded that He mercifully extends grace to me because He loves me, not for *how* I am but for *who* I am. I am His child.

What adjectives best describe you on your worst days? Are you: merciful, gracious, not easily angered and loving or, like me, do you sometimes nag, scold and hold grudges?

I have such a long way to go on my spiritual journey. And it's not a journey that can be made in a box with the help of a U.P.S. man. I'm so glad you and I are traveling together.

On days when I feel like I'm making no progress, I am encouraged by Saint Paul and young Saint Timothy who reassure me in * Philippians 1:6 that:

"God who started this great work in you
would keep at it and bring it to a flourishing finish
on the very day Christ Jesus appears."

This Scripture is meant for us today every bit as much as the people in Philippi. Saint Paul and Saint Timothy are praying for us knowing that God will bring us to a "flourishing finish" in our pursuit of holiness.

Do you sometimes doubt yourself? I do. At times I feel like

I'll always be stuck in the mud, frustrated and forever confessing the same sins of impatience and an unrestrained tongue. But even though we feel stuck **down**, God is willing to lift us **up**. He's all about **UP's**, so while He is certainly not employed by U.P.S., He wants to help. We just need to turn to Him.

Turning to Him first (rather than last) is a lesson I'm still learning. Sometimes I turn to food in frustration or to Facebook. Sometimes I turn to a friend who will listen to me gripe. To what or whom do you turn?

THE JOURNEY FORWARD:

My daughter insists she is correct and that the nice man in brown clothes who gives us packages is the P.U.S. man. Like Alyssa, sometimes I get things a bit out of order too.

On your journey forward today, instead of trying to package problems and ship them off, break them down like you would break down a cardboard box and take them to the feet of your Father.

LENT WAS THE PITS

$\mathcal{A}$s a child, how did you celebrate Easter? What are some of your favorite traditions and memories? For me as a kid, Easter was second only to Christmas.

We had the forty days of Lent to anticipate all the goodies the Easter bunny would leave us in our baskets. The day before Ash Wednesday we would swallow every sweet in sight in desperate preparation for forty days of denial.

Lent was the pits.

We would count the days until Easter morning when we would bounce out of bed before the first ray would dance through the drapes in the front room. Light was not a necessity for the Nale crew. We had our game plan formulated.

Mom always bought chocolate from Bidwell's Candy Store. It was a small family-owned shop just a few blocks away. You know the sort. When you walked in the door, you could taste the creamy aroma of sweet delights.

They had everything you could fathom and free samples to boot. The best part was sitting at the delicate scalloped tables with red and white tablecloths.

But one Easter was different. Instead of shopping at Bidwell's, Mom bought everything at the GNC–the General Nutrition Center. She crammed our baskets full of nutritious candy. "Nutritious" and "candy" did not belong in the same sentence, not to mention in our Easter baskets.

It seemed to us a crazy coup to overthrow the existing tradition of real candy.

Carob bunnies lead the invasion.

Carob-covered raisins dropped from eggs like grenades.

Carob-covered nuts catapulted from colored chicks.

Fruit roll ups were aimed at us liked cannons. Granola bars sunk beneath the surface like submarines and bags of trail mix was scattered everywhere amidst the pastel, plastic grass like shrapnel. Why, we couldn't even trade the healthy stuff with our cousin Kimmy for green jelly beans.

Our outcry was deafening.

That was the only Easter that my mother waged war on chocolate bunnies. Now and again, she attempted to slip a few raisins into our cookies disguised as chocolate chips. She even used honey incognito in our morning oatmeal and put wheat germ in our pancakes. But we had diplomatically secured a peace treaty outlining Easter's need to be celebrated with real candy.

After fasting for forty long days and forty long nights we wanted real chocolate...and lots of it!

With Lent being just around the corner, many folks are trying to decide what they will give up denying their flesh with spiritual growth being the goal. But does God want us to deny ourselves?

Is He pleased if we abstain from something that we enjoy? Would He want us to do without? Should we go so far as to actually fast? And what purpose would it serve?

Jesus Himself fasted.

We read in Matthew 4 that immediately after He was baptized by John in the Jordan He was taken by Satan to the dessert to be tested. Jesus prepared Himself for this trial by fasting forty nights and days, which left Him in an extreme state of hunger. Though He must have lacked physical strength, He was spiritually strong. He resisted Satan not once, or twice, but three times.

If we are to interpret Scripture literally, this means Jesus went without food for nearly six weeks. Can you imagine going without food for even one week? Honestly, I struggle to deny myself one meal.

Imagine how weak He must have felt. Even walking must have been a chore. Did you ever wonder why the Bible says that He fasted for forty days and nights?

Forty is a number representing completion. The first time

God destroyed the earth, it rained for forty days and nights. Every living creature that was not inside Noah's ark was completely destroyed. Hundreds of years later, the Hebrew nation wandered in the desert for forty years before crossing the Jordan into the Promised Land.

Forty is the number of years required to complete a generation. Again, hundreds of years later after Jesus had risen from the dead, He stayed forty days before He ascended into heaven.

While on earth, Jesus had the most powerful ministry ever recorded. We gain some insight into the source of this power. His disciples came to Him distressed because they were unable to cast out the evil spirit. Jesus simply commanded the spirit to be gone and it was. When His disciples asked Him later in private why they were not successful, He answered in **Mark 9:29:

"This kind can come forth by nothing,
but by prayer and fasting."

Prayer and fasting fit together, hand and glove. Denying the flesh can serve to strengthen the spirit. The two can be linked. If time that is normally spent feeding our bodies is spent instead feeding our spirits, wouldn't we be spiritually renewed and strengthened?

The goal is for our flesh to submit to our spirit, which is aligned with His Spirit. If we would die to self, could we live as a more powerful example of grace? Would we see more **wonder**? I think so.

This leads me to ask myself: Which is stronger, my flesh or my spirit? For me, it depends on the day...even the time of day. Which would you like to reign?

Jesus had put His flesh to death long before He ever arrived at Golgotha. He taught both in word and deed. Concerning fasting, He summarized for His apostles in *Matthew 6:16-18 saying that when they denied themselves food, they needed to concentrate on God without making a production out of it which would draw attention:

"It might turn you into a small-time celebrity,
but it won't make you a saint.
If you 'go into training' inwardly,
act normal outwardly."

Then Jesus tells them to wash their hair, brush their teeth and scrub their faces. God knows that they are fasting, and He will reward them. So, we can see from these passages that fasting is a spiritual discipline, much like prayer.

The disciples understood the role of fasting from Jesus. We see in Acts 13:2 this spiritual discipline alongside worship and prayer. The disciples were worshipping God and fasting as they waited for the Holy Spirit to direct them in ministry.

The Spirit prompted them to commission both Paul and Barnabas for evangelism. Again after spreading the Good News making many disciples in Derbe, they returned to Lystra, Iconium, and Antioch of Pisidia, where they encouraged believers. They reminded them that together they must suffer many trials to enter the Kingdom of God. Paul and Barnabas also appointed elders in every church.

With prayer and fasting, they turned the elders over to the care of the Lord, in whom they had put their trust (Acts 14:21-23). The Bible gives us a rich understanding of how and when we can fast.

If you feel led by the Spirit to fast (cleared by your physician of course), perhaps you could start by skipping one meal. Maybe you would choose to fast from sweets for a day. I've heard of some folks fasting from Starbucks.

While in my third year of pharmacy school, I fasted from "Fast Food" during Lent. These days I am less creative choosing to fast from solids, drinking only milk to maintain energy. The type of fast is not as important as the heart attitude. Is this something that you can do with someone like minded? I have found that challenges are always easier when faced with a friend.

Those who are Catholic, grew up together abstaining from meat on Fridays during Lent. People in my parish would come together every Friday night for fish fries sponsored by the Knights of Columbus. It was a way to raise money for needy children, while abstaining from meat in preparation and anticipation of Easter.

If you feel led to fast and pray, I would recommend the book *Fast Friends: The Amazing Power of Friendship, Fasting and Prayer* by Suzanne Niles and Wendy Simpson Little.

THE JOURNEY FORWARD:

The decision to fast is a personal one, but I do have an exercise I would like to purpose on our journey today. Could you *fast* from eating *fast*, slowing down enough today to savor the flavor of each wonderful bite?

Perhaps you could put down your utensils between mouthfuls? Be **wowed** like a kid on Easter morning who nibbles slowly on milk chocolate bunny ears.

THE LITTLE ENGINE THAT COULD

"I think I can. I think I can. I think I can."

Do you remember the **wonder-filled** story of *The Little Engine That Could*? On her way to deliver a cargo of magical toys to eagerly waiting children, Georgia, the engine, suddenly breaks down.

Pete, the powerful freight engine, and Farnsworth, the shiny passenger engine, refuse to help. Rusty old Zebadiah is just too worn out, but a little switch engine named Tillie thinks she can do it.

My daughter enjoys this story as I did. For generations, children have learned about hard work and putting others first. They have been **wowed** as they cheered for the little engine that could and did.

THOUGH YEARS HAVE PASSED, AND YOU MAY HAVE LONG forgotten Tillie's name, the book provided a **Window of Wonder** moment today like never before when I read it to my daughter.

After she drifted off to sleep, I thought about how the story continues to provide a framework for us as Christians to learn about the saving power of Christ.

As believers, our indelible rallying cry can similarly inspire and be even more positive than that of the little engine. There is no element of doubt about our ability to accomplish God's Will through Christ for we are told by Jesus Himself in Luke 18:27:

"The things which are impossible with men
are possible with God."

This was Jesus' response to the question from His disciples who asked how anyone could be "good enough" to be saved. Through Christ the impossible feat of salvation becomes possible. We don't have the power to save ourselves, which is why we need a Savior.

We are told in Romans 8:37 that through Christ we become more than conquerors, as we are victors over sin and spiritual death. Our salvation is secure in Christ. Even in death, we are not defeated. Since with God all things are possible, our rallying cry as believers can be:

"With God I can. With God I can. With God I can."

He reassures us that every detail in our lives can be worked into something good (Romans 8:28). God did not say that every detail is good. Sickness is not good. Violence is not good. Abuse is not good. Can you think of other examples of things in life that are not good?

But God promises us believers that He can and will use even those things that are "not good" to "bring good." Has God ever brought good out of a circumstance that was not good? If so, your life stands as a testimony to others on their journey. Have you shared your witness?

If you are in the middle of a trial that is "not good," it is easy to become discouraged. We can become weary like rusty old Zebadiah in the story of *The Little Engine that Could.* You and I can have moments of doubt. But if doubts persist, Paul reminds us in* Romans 8:31b:

"If God is for us, who can ever be against us?"

When our will is aligned with God's will, there is no challenge too great for us who believe in Christ. Like the little engine, we are told that we will face challenges in this life. In John 16:33 we are reminded:

"Here on earth you **will** have **many** trials and sorrows.
But take heart, because I have overcome the world."

This verse makes it clear that being Christian does not exempt us from hardships. It is a difficult passage. Point blank, we are guaranteed trials...many trials. We will walk "thru" the valley of the shadow of death (Psalm 23:4). Quite honestly, I would rather go *around* the valley of death...or glide *above* it. But, if I have to go *thru* it, I can think of no one better to guide me than Christ, Who has conquered death. He's *been there, done that* and wants to help me do the same.

There is no situation that His Spirit cannot improve. We are told that in *Romans 8:32-34 without hesitation God put everything on the line for us, embracing our sinfulness and exposing Himself to the worst. There isn't anything He wouldn't willingly do for us:

> "And who would dare tangle with God
> by messing with one of God's chosen?
> Who would dare even to point a finger?
> The One who died for us
> —who was raised to life for us!—
> is in the presence of God at this very moment
> sticking up for us."

Does it amaze you to think that Jesus is in God's presence "sticking up for us" being our advocate and coming to our defense?

He continues on in verse 35-37 asking if we think that anyone is going to be able to "drive a wedge" between us and God's love? Paul says that's not going to happen:

> "Not trouble, not hard times, not hatred, not hunger,

not homelessness, not bullying threats, not backstabbing,
not even the worst sins listed in Scripture
will separate us from Christ's love.
No, despite all these things, overwhelming victory is ours
through Christ, who loved us."

Christ is cheering us on this very moment in the presence of God.

"He knows we can. He knows we can. He knows we can."

With the fast pace of life in America, stress is common. Tribulation is prevalent and persecution possible. Spiritual famine is widespread. Peril plagues our cities, while swords have been replaced by revolvers and rifles in our country. Yet with all the confusion, we can be reassured that:

"With God we can. With God we can. With God we can."

As believers, the title of *The Little Engine That Could* might well be changed to *The Little Christian That Could*, based on the promise of Philippians 4:13:

"For I can do everything through Christ,
who gives me strength."

THE JOURNEY FORWARD:

Today instead of repeating:

"I think I can. I think I can. I think I can"

as you chug along the track of your daily routine aligned with God's Will, you and I can provide others with a **W.O.W.** moment living out the truth:

"**In Christ we can. In Christ we can. In Christ we can.**"

KING ME!

I have never been able to **wow** and win anyone at the game of checkers, and I am simply atrocious when it comes to the game of chess. I am still trying to remember whether the rookie moves forward and to the left or to the right. The pawns are just about my speed, loyally plodding along one square at a time.

I don't naturally strategize. Unlike my husband who enjoys the mental gymnastics, I don't think it is fun to ponder the position of the players. I crave more immediate results. I want to arrive at the other side of the game board and experience the gratification of being able to holler, "KING ME!" Call me child-like, but I do like to win and be rewarded. How about you?

Today Alyssa asked me to play checkers. Her favorite part was jumping her checkers unrestrained all over the board and then jumping herself all around the room. Rules didn't restrict her zest to enthusiastically bounce her red checkers to the far side.

It must be genetic because my little Alyssa loved to bellow out a big "KING ME" when she safely arrived at the opposite side. Even our cat Truffles had to come investigate the commotion.

AS I ADMIRED ALYSSA'S EXCITEMENT AND **WONDER**, I WAS **WOWED** by how much life and the game of checkers have in common. Someday you and I will arrive at the other side of this "game of life." Much like in the game of checkers, when we stand before the throne of our King He will "king" us by placing a crown on our heads. Just the thought **wows** me and make me hungry to learn more.

So today in my **hunger for wonder**, I studied about scriptural "crowns." Can you hike alongside me today? I learned that there are eight references in the New Testament that provide a window through which we can view the **wonder** of the crowns promised to us.

The first reference is found in **1 Corinthians 9:24-25 where Paul equates life to a race rather than to a game of checkers. He explains saying that everyone is running, but only one person wins first place. He tells us to run all out, disciplining ourselves like athletes so that we can win the grand prize saying:

"Now they do it to obtain a corruptible crown;

but we an incorruptible."

When your feet hit the floor each morning, do you see each day as a sacred race? Are you running to finish in first place, or do you simply want to make it across the finish line at the end of the day? Oftentimes I find that my spirit is willing to sprint, but my flesh wants to walk. I want to finish strong, but I grow weary.

By the time I cross the finish line at 11:00 p.m., I am exhausted. If you find yourself fatigued, be encouraged and strengthened by knowing that a crown waits for you at the end of this life that is checkered with diversions and frustrations. The younger brother of Jesus tells us in James 1:12:

"God blesses those who patiently endure
testing and temptation.
Afterward they will receive the crown of life
that God has promised to those who love him."

Not only did Saint Paul and Saint James write concerning incorruptible crowns, Saint Peter also reinforces the existence of these crowns in 1 Peter 5:4:

"And when the Great Shepherd appears,
you will receive a crown of never-ending glory and honor."

Finally, in the book of Revelation crowns are mentioned five times, twice with reference to our crowns as servants of the

Lord. Saint John speaks on behalf of the Lord in Revelation 3:11 where it is written:

> "I am coming soon.
> Hold on to what you have,
> so that no one will take away your crown."

From this passage, we know that crowns are a separate entity and not to be confused with or equated to eternal life, for in John 6:27 we are told that our salvation is sealed by God the Father Himself.

As we **hunger for wonder** today, we learned about heavenly crowns. Though we do not know exactly what those crowns will be like, the eight Scripture references in the New Testament do provide us with a window through which we can gaze at the **wonder** that awaits us.

We have read about the incorruptible crown, the crown of righteousness, the crown of life, and the crown of glory. It's amazing to think that Our Lord would want to reward us with crowns.

It speaks to me of His love for us. It also humbles me because I know that He alone is worthy of a crown. He alone wore a crown of thorns for me. Our goal in this checkered "game of life" is not to amass heavenly crowns, but rather to bring Him glory.

THE JOURNEY FORWARD:

For today's journey glance through Scripture's **window into the wonder** of Philippians 4:1 and notice what St. Paul says about you?

> "I love you and long to see you, dear friends,
> for you are my joy
> and the **crown** I receive for my work."

AIRPLANES

*H*ave you ever wondered how aircrafts actually fly? As I sit in a 747 on the tarmac *with my seat belt fastened and my seat back and folding trays in their full and upright position*, I ponder this question.

It is amazing to me that a huge chunk of metal filled with people can actually be suspended in air. It may seem that the law of gravity is being broken but I know it's not. I understand that the law of gravity still exists, but if I remember correctly, the laws of aerodynamics also come into play. Before I turn off my laptop for the flight, I quickly search "How do planes fly?" to refresh my memory.

Aerodynamics is the way air moves around things. The rules of aerodynamics explain how something so heavy, like a metal jet, is able to be suspended by something so light, like air.

I read about the four forces of weight, lift, thrust and drag.

Everything has weight due to gravity pulling objects down to Earth. To fly, an aircraft needs something to lift it in the opposite direction from gravity. The larger the weight, the larger this lift needs to be.

Lift comes from the shape of a planes wings that are curved on the top and flatter on the bottom. This shape makes air flow over the top faster than under the bottom. So, less air pressure is on top of the wing, allowing the wing and the attached airplane to move up.

Thrust and drag are also forces that come into play. Thrust is the force that moves something forward while drag is the force that tries to slow things down. For an aircraft to keep moving forward, it must have more thrust than drag.

While a small airplane gets its thrust from a propeller, a large 747 needs jets. Together all these forces seem to defy the law of gravity, when they actually don't.

Now I can both feel and hear the power of the jet engines as we start to pick up speed down the runway. My head is thrust into the chair back. On life off, there is a singular moment in time when the wheels no longer touch the pavement. This is my **W.O.W.** moment.

What was once thought impossible is now possible. What once seemed extra-ordinary is now ordinary. I close my eyes and soak in the **wonder**.

THERE IS AN AMAZING SPIRITUAL LESSON TO BE CAUGHT EACH TIME

we catch a flight. Just as planes seem to defy the law of gravity, some of Jesus' New Testament teachings seem to defy the laws of the Old Testament. Have you ever noticed this?

It can be perplexing. But the law is never erased as Jesus explains in Matthew 5:18-19 when He tells us not to suppose for a second that He came to demolish any part of God's Law or the Laws of the Prophets.

He tells us His purpose is to fulfill the Law. Then He shares that those who obey God's Laws and teach others to do likewise will be considered great in God's kingdom. Those who ignore the Law and teach others to do likewise will be considered the least in His kingdom.

There are times when Christ beckons us to a "higher calling." This higher calling in no way diminishes the original law, just as a plane taking off does not negate the law of gravity. Jesus Himself gives us an example of this paradox explaining in *Matthew 5:38:

"Here's another old saying that deserves a second look:
'Eye for eye, tooth for tooth.'
Is that going to get us anywhere?
Here's what I propose: 'Don't hit back at all.'"

At first this appears to be a contradiction. It may seem that Jesus is saying that His law of turning the other cheek abolishes or erases the law of repayment that says the loss of an eye *could* be repaid by the loss of the eye of the offender (Leviticus 24:20). The law of repayment is not abolished. We are simply lifted–much as a plane is lifted–to a higher standard.

As Christians, we are to glide above the world of revenge. We are to soar as examples of kindness. We are to repay evil with goodness. We are to love others extending grace and mercy, even when they seem unlovable.

This is hard for me. How about you? Jesus is very adamant and very down-to-earth. He gives us three practical examples of "higher callings" found in Matthew 5:40-42:

"If you are sued in court and your shirt is taken from you,
give your coat, too.
If a soldier demands that you carry his gear for a mile,
carry it two miles.
Give to those who ask,
and don't turn away from those who want to borrow."

In Biblical times, the Holy Land was under Roman authority. By law, any Jew if asked by a Roman soldier to carry his load must oblige. Not only was this physically difficult, it was demeaning. In verse 41, Jesus is urging Christians to carry things twice the distance. Imagine carrying heavy supplies a full two miles.

I remember having to carry groceries nine blocks back to my dorm when I was in undergrad. A mere liter of pop became an incredible burden as the blocks wore on. Weight took on a whole new perspective.

Jesus is challenging us to do more than love our friends and hate our enemies. He tells us to love our enemies letting them bring out the best in us rather than the worst.

He tells us to pray for those who give us a hard time. In giving others our best, we are following God's example Who gives His best. He gives us sun to warm us and rain to nourish us regardless of our worthiness. Anyone can hate their enemies, but we are called in *Matthew 5:48 to:

> "Live out your God-created identity.
> Live generously and graciously toward others,
> the way God lives toward you."

To extend grace and mercy is our higher calling. Over the years I have heard many preachers say that grace gives people what they *do not deserve*. Mercy does not give people what *they do deserve*. I can read it, but to live it, that's hard.

THE JOURNEY FORWARD:

So, like a plane flying seems to defy gravity, some of Jesus's New Testament teachings on grace and mercy seem to defy the Old Testament Laws. While we don't face social injustices imposed by Roman rule in America, we still have opportunities to practice grace and mercy.

Instead of carrying a Roman soldier's burdensome gear on foot, we may be given the opportunity to help carry another's emotional burdens. We may be able to help a person through the loss of a loved one, a divorce or an illness. We may be called on to carry a colleague's workload.

If so, Jesus asks us to literally "go the extra mile." Will you go above and beyond the next time a person asks you for help? I'll give it my best if you will.

THE "MIRACLE" OF THE FISH

*M*y Dad was good at a lot of things, but he was not a fisherman, so when I was nine and my brother five, my Mom took us fishing. She thought it would be a day filled with **wonder** making memories.

Grandpa had given us each our own fishing pole from his collection just for the occasion. He had also given us a brief casting lesson in the alley near the railroad tracks. He cautioned us not to let the lines tangle and under no circumstances were we to get the reels wet.

So–stink bait and worms in tow–we headed toward Lake Paradise and the fishing ponds nearby. We were so excited. We wiggled more than the worms!

Once at the ponds we wasted no time and chose the first spot, which happened to be near an intake pipe with a motor-driven pump that moved water between two smaller ponds. The pump was covered by a wooden ramp that sloped down into the water.

My brother wanted to fish on one side and I wanted to fish on the other. At the time it seemed like a good idea as it would separate us, and our lines wouldn't tangle together.

Mom ran between us replenishing our hooks as we reeled in the algae. Now Brian–despite being told to walk around the ramp when he wanted more worms–liked taking the dangerous short cut. He would crawl over the ramp, ignoring my mother's warning that he might slide down into the water.

Brian was the first to get a bite.

He shouted in glee.

Mom cheered.

I jumped up and down in joy.

We all tugged hard as we reeled that rascal to shore.

It was a communal effort.

Boy, were we surprised to discover it weighed less than all the worms we had lost and measured about five inches in length. We weren't disappointed though. Much to the contrary, we were proud. Mom said we would have it for dinner. Now it was my turn to catch one. Mom was baiting my hook when...

SPLASH!

My little brother slid down the ramp and disappeared into the dark pond. My mom dropped the plastic jar of stink bait on my flip-flopped foot and galloped full stride down the steep slope picking up speed as she strode.

SPLASH!

She was swimming toward my brother. At least I assumed it was Barney. All I could see was his fishing pole sticking straight out of the water pointing toward heaven and circling as if to sing "Here I am Lord. It is I Lord."

My mother dragged my brother—who was still obediently holding his reel out of the water—toward shore. I was immobilized, not with fear, but with laughter. The sight of that fishing pole bobbing vertically in the breeze just poked my funny bone.

Mom begged me to come pull my brother out, as she couldn't stand, and the edge was steep and muddy. She was fearful as she could hear the blades of the motor chipping away and feel the current sucking water toward the large intake tunnel.

The more she pleaded, the harder I laughed. I didn't mean to be defiant, but the whole scene just seemed hysterical. I didn't understand the risk.

When Mom did finally get Brian out, she hugged and kissed him, asking over and over again if he was okay. He spit pureed algae water out of his mouth and replied in a rather matter of fact tone, "Yup. But it sure was dark down there."

Our. Fishing. Excursion. Was. Over.

Dripping wet, Brian oozed mud. We both piled in the car as Mom, shivering, threw our gear in the trunk. We headed home. Mom thanked God aloud that Brian wasn't pulled under and sucked through the fan blades of the motor. Brian thanked God that his prized fishing reel wasn't wet and I...well...the stench of the stink bait between my flip flopped toes filled the car, as did my laughter.

Five hours later, I was still giggling. As we sat around the dinner table, we prayed. Then Mom recounted the story to Dad and my older sister, Kathy. Barney beamed. At five years old, his five-inch fish fed our entire family of five. We even had left-overs. Ah, the **wonder** of the moment.

THAT FIVE-INCH FISH PROBABLY WEIGHED FIVE OUNCES DRIPPING wet. Does something sound fishy to you? Or does it remind you of the miracle when Jesus fed 5,000? Matthew, Mark, Luke and John each provide us with the same important details of Jesus using two fish and five loaves of bread to feed 5,000 men, not counting women and children.

Before we read about those details, I think it's important to know that Jesus had just received news that His cousin—John the Baptist—had been beheaded by Herod Antipas. Jesus had grown up with His cousin, who was just six months older than Him; in all likelihood, they had gone fishing together just as Barney and me. Jesus must have been very sad, don't you think?

What do you do first when you receive horrific news? If you're like me, you probably want to spend time with those you love, as you try to grapple with the loss. That is exactly what Jesus wanted as we learn in Mark 6:31-34 when Jesus said:

"'Let's go off by ourselves to a quiet place and rest awhile.'"

There were so many people coming and going that the apostles and Jesus didn't even have time to eat. We learn they left "for a quiet place." But crowds recognized them, seeing them leaving. They followed them running ahead along the shoreline as the apostles headed across the water.

When their boat did finally arrive, and Jesus stepped to shore, a large group of people had already gathered, waiting for Him. We learn that He had compassion on them as they reminded Him of sheep with no shepherd.

If you are a parent, you understand the need for time alone. Yet you also understand that your children have needs. They need to eat. When you meet those needs having compassion for them, you resemble Jesus. Though He was mourning and tired, Jesus had compassion and put the spiritual and physical needs of the crowd before His own physical and emotional needs.

We pick up the story learning that later in the afternoon His disciples came to Him concerned because they were far from a place where the throng of people could buy food. The disciples wanted Jesus to dismiss everyone so they could go to the nearby farms and villages but Jesus said in verse 37-38 we learn:

But Jesus replied in matter of fact tone,
'You feed them.'
They were astonished responding
'We'd have to work for months to earn enough money
to buy food for all these people!'"

That's when Jesus had them take inventory of their own

supply asking how much food that actually did have. They reported back:

"We have five loaves of bread and two fish."

Have you ever had less than you needed, and you needed God to show up? I sure have, and He multiplied the little that I had. We learn how the story ends in verses 39-43 when Jesus told the multitude to sit down on the grass in groups. They obeyed clustering in groups of fifty to one hundred.

Then Jesus took the bread and fish and looked to His Father blessing the food. He broke the bread into pieces, passing it to His disciples to share with the hungry people. He did likewise with the fish. Then we learn:

"They all ate as much as they wanted, and afterward,
the disciples picked up twelve baskets of leftover bread and fish.
A total of 5,000 men and their families were fed."

Every gospel writer makes sure to tell us there were lots of leftovers. While my family is not big on leftovers, the reason this is so important is that this miracle was performed for 5,000 non-Jewish men and their families.

Jesus wanted the Jewish people to know that there was plenty to feed them also. One basket for each of the twelve tribes of Israel remained. None go hungry when they come to Jesus.

So when we come to Him as we **hunger for wonder**, He feeds us by asking us to give Him what we have. He wants our *ordinary* five loaves and two fish abilities. He wants our five loaves and two fish moments. Our talents and our time in His hands can make a difference. It may not seem like much compared to the need, but He starts with the *ordinary*.

He never asks for more than you and I have, but He wants you and I to trust Him to multiply what we have to meet what others need. He makes the *ordinary, extra-ordinary*. And sometimes, like with this miracle, the ordinary became *extraordinary* right before their eyes.

Oftentimes, like the apostles, I am so busy I don't notice the miracle in front of me until I glance up and see all the baskets of blessings that are "leftover." What do you have that you can share? What do you need most today?

When my brother was five and I was nine, we experienced a fishing expedition that sounds vaguely like that of Jesus' miracle with the loaves and fishes...only a few variables were different.

The setting wasn't near the Sea of Galilee outside Bethsaida but rather Lake Paradise outside Mattoon, a mid-western town of 18,000. We had only one fish; Jesus had two.

In our story, one fish fed a family of five, rather than a crowd of over 5,000. The protagonist wasn't our Lord but my Mother (with the help of the local grocer). And the real miracle was not the multiplication of fish, but the safety of my little brother and the **wonder** we discovered that day.

THE JOURNEY FORWARD:

Do you have your menu planned for dinner tonight? Might you have fish in the freezer? If so, why not make fish for dinner and have a conversation with your family about this miracle and how it can apply to their lives. What *five loaves and two fish* do they have that can be multiplied to help others? Do they trust Jesus to help them?

ARE YOU SLEEPY?

"*A*re you sleepy?" Have you found that there is only one answer to this question...if you ask a toddler? Despite their fatigue, they find the energy to offer a vigorous "No."

Even as my daughter drifts into a slumber, she refuses to admit she's drowsy. However, tonight she conceded to her Daddy, "My head is tired...but I'm not." When Dave asked if she wanted to go to bed, she retorted, "But I'm not sleepy, only my eyes are tired."

SLEEPY JUST ISN'T A WORD IN ALYSSA'S VOCABULARY. I HUNGER **for the wonder** of a toddler who is so interested and engaged in life, they don't want to sleep for a moment. Do you have that same **hunger for wonder**?

We are more than one third of the way through our journey and we are picking up speed. Yet as I sit with my Bible, I often find that I am physically sleepy even though I am called to be spiritually alert.

In Matthew 24:42-44 Jesus advises us to "keep watch" because we don't know when He will return. He explains that if homeowners knew what day a burglar was coming, they would guard their house, so it wouldn't be robbed.

Likewise, He tells us that we should be ready because He will return when we least expect it. Are you ready? Somedays, I am prepared, other days…well, I am sleepy.

Then in verse 45, Jesus explains that those who watch for His return—as a servant would watch for the return of his master—will be rewarded by being put in charge of all his master's possessions. Hmm…imagine that. If we are faithful and wise managers, the Lord will put us in charge of more of His possessions.

Those who are good stewards of what riches and responsibilities they are given will be given more riches and responsibilities. This catches my attention. Just as Jesus reminds us through parables to be awake, Peter also delivers a similar message. He says that we shouldn't take anything for granted because everything in the world is about be "wrapped up."

He tells us to stay wide-awake in prayer. But most importantly we are to love each other as if our lives depended on it because love makes up for practically anything. He gives us examples of how to love others by being cheerfully quick to offer a meal to the hungry or a bed to the homeless. He tells us in*1 Peter 4:7-11 to be generous with the gifts we have been given so that:

> "God's bright presence
> will be evident in everything through Jesus,
> and he'll get all the credit
> as the One mighty in everything—
> encores to the end of time."

Do you love others like your life depended on it living every day, reaching out to others in love as Jesus did when He was on earth? Are we living as we would if Jesus where here with us or are we wandering as if we were sleepwalking through life? Paul is straightforward, not mincing words when he says in *1 Thessalonians 5:6,8:

> "So let's not sleepwalk through life like those others.
> Let's keep our eyes open and be smart.
> Walk out into the daylight sober,
> dressed up in faith, love, and the hope of salvation."

As a child, I would sleep walk right out the back door and down the alley toward my friend, Susie Stuckey's house. Because the storm door never locked securely, my mom would pile the kitchen chairs in front of the door. That way, she could hear me before I escaped out the door. So while I physically outgrew sleep walking, I'm still growing spiritually learning to walk with Him fully engaged.

THE JOURNEY FORWARD:

Though my daughter's head may be tired, and her eyes may be sleepy, she wants to keep watch. A child's simple desire to stay awake can provide a **W.O.W.** moment that reveals a deeper spiritual truth.

As sojourners who **hunger for wonder** we too are called to stay alert. So before you close your eyes tonight, could you read about bridesmaids in Matthew 25:1-13?

ETCH A SKETCH

*A*ll I can say is "**wow**" after visiting the toy aisle at Walmart. It's an experience in technology. There are toy laptop computers that talk to you, teach you your colors, your numbers, and your ABC's.

There are toy cellphones to link the upwardly mobile tricycle tykes with Big Wheel® riders in the world of corporate chaos. And after a hard day at the sandbox, kids can come home to their own TV remote controls that have more confusing buttons than mine.

Amidst the aisles of whirling gismos and gadgets, there are a few bastions of tradition. Hidden in a remote corner is a box full of Hula Hoops®. Even the words +96 "Hula Hoop" are fun to say fast, though that is about all I can still do fast with a Hula Hoop. Without practice, all the hula has gone out of my hoop.

But you never forget how to use an Etch A Sketch®. The

simplicity of two dials is wonderfully refreshing. One dial moves the line up and down, the other moves the line side to side.

For the advanced "Etch A Sketcher," you can move both the dials at once to make cool spirals. Trapezoids, squares, rectangles, triangles, circles, and even rhombuses appear before your very eyes. No batteries needed. Stop counting the required bytes. The Etch A Sketch is fueled by metal shavings and a modest magnet.

But what I like best about the Etch A Sketch is that you can shake it once real hard, and all the mess is erased. It simply disappears. Which is why our **W.O.W.** moment today is brought to you by Etch A Sketch.

WOULDN'T IT BE NICE IF LIFE WERE AS SIMPLE TO CLEAN UP AND mistakes could be erased with one shake? Though the Etch A Sketch is elementary, it has a complex lesson to teach us about the spiritual world—a message about powers of darkness which are as numerous as the metal shavings inside an Etch A Sketch.

Just as the shavings are hidden from view, so are the spiritual forces of wickedness. In Ephesians 6:12, Paul explains:

"For we are not fighting against flesh-and-blood enemies,
but against evil rulers and authorities of the unseen world,
against mighty powers in this dark world,
and against evil spirits in the heavenly places."

Indeed, there is a demonic force at work in the world, as assuredly as there is a magnetic force at work in an Etch A Sketch. But instead of innocently drawing doodles as we did in childhood, evil is drawing havoc and death in people's lives.

Though the thought is unsettling, we are fighting an external spiritual battle every day with the world, while we are internally waging war with our flesh as we seek to walk in the Spirit. Do you ever feel these forces at work or see their effects on the news?

No matter how grim things look, how much sin darkens our world or how much sickness robs us of our loved ones, we know that Jesus has defeated sin and death by giving His life understanding *1 Corinthians 15:55:

> "Death swallowed by triumphant Life!
> Who got the last word, oh, Death?
> Oh, Death, who's afraid of you now?"

I love St. Paul's simple poetic summary, but I know that it was far from simple for Jesus to die. It's also far from simple to come to accept the death of someone we love. It's even difficult to think about our own death.

When I was younger, the thought of the end of the world and death was haunting. But God has slowly helped me to fully grasp death's defeat by Christ and something amazing has happened. I'm no longer afraid. Fear has been replaced by peace and I can truly say fear of death has been swallowed by Life!

THE JOURNEY FORWARD:

I love the simplicity of the magnetic Etch-A-Sketch and I love the simplicity of the magnetic message of salvation. Not only does our Savior save us from death, but He also saves us from the *fear of* death.

Know that you are not alone if you are fearful or anxious, but also know that you can trust your Savior. When fear of death threatens your thoughts, look to Jesus. Give those fears to the One who looked Death eye to eye and delivered the knock-out punch!

BLUE CAKE WITH GREEN ICING

WANTS VS. NEEDS

*D*ecisions. Decisions. Decisions. My sweet Alyssa turns three next month. She welcomes the world through such eyes of excited **wonder.** This morning when she saw a birthday cake on Sesame Street, I told her she could have any kind of cake she wanted.

She bounced up and down with her first choice bubbling out of her mouth as her arms shot up. "I want a blue cake with green icing just like Big Bird." Every half hour since, she has changed her mind on what color of cake she "needs."

Her sense of excited **wonder** has blurred together like the blue, green, purple and red colors she has chosen throughout the day forming this brown, blurry blob of discontentment. A sense of obsession has replaced her whimsical **wonder.** The color of her cake is less relevant to me than her repeated choice of verb and increasing intensity which has caught my attention.

I would like her to be able to distinguish a need from a want. Like Alyssa, I too can confuse needs and wants. It's easy to do when those around us may have their needs and wants confused.

Today the Kansas City Star Sunday paper carried a two-page layout on the lack of financial security in America. The whole point, as the headline indicated, was that Americans were sick and tired and mad. They wanted more prosperity.

Hmm...This is a paradox as the average family owns more cars, more telephones, more televisions and lives in larger and newer homes than ever before in the history of this country.

The content of the headlines tells us that America is not content. Do some confuse their wants and needs? Does my daughter *need* a blue cake with green icing? Nope, but she sure *wants* it. In fact, it dominates her thoughts like a big bully.

WANTS VS. NEEDS. THE SUBJECT IS AS STICKY AS THE GREEN ICING my daughter craves. Let me just say now that we are made to crave. But do these cravings for things satisfy our **hunger for wonder** and our need for a Savior?

Craving comes quite naturally for our flesh. I certainly don't have to force myself to eat cake. I want it. And, while we are on the subject let me say for the record, I want my ice-cream too. Chocolate chip cookie dough, please.

The issue is when Alyssa and I attempt to satiate our cravings with things that were never meant to fill us full. Do you ever crave things that don't fulfill you? The first of the Ten Commandments found in Exodus 20:3 is:

"You must not have any other god but me."

My Creator made me, and He knows that I crave relationships. But He tells me that He is to have first place in my heart. There shall be no other gods before Him. Do you find that often as women or men, we crave relationships so desperately that our hearts are willing to stuff anyone with a pulse into God's rightful position? Sometimes that someone is not healthy themselves.

Jesus summarized all His Dad's rules with two sentences. In Mark 12:30-31 we read that we are to love the Lord our God with our entire being, and love our neighbor as our self. There you have it. That is God's order. **Love Him. Love others.**

Yes, we are made to crave a companion and friends, but they will never satiate the primary need for God in our lives. Nor will riches satiate the need for God or companions. It is the act of putting people before God or our riches before relationships that causes the problems.

Relationships and riches themselves are certainly not evil. Like God desires a relationship with us, we too desire relationships. The Bible is very clear when it comes to material possessions.

St. Paul warns us in Hebrews 13:5 to stay away from "the love of money" and be content with what we have. It is this love of money that Jesus takes issue with. We are to love Him first, then others.

We are never to love things. Clean and simple. But I can make things so sticky and messy, like all different colors of icing mixed together.

We complicate life when we love our cravings and stuff more than God. That being said, our Father clearly understands that we do have needs. The need for daily bread is the first thing we are told to ask for when His Son teaches us to pray in the "Our Father." But God doesn't stop there.

Close to 2,000 Scriptures address wealth in God's Word. There are 101 Proverbs alone on the subject (Yup. I counted.). There are forty-six parables that Jesus told, half dealt with money. God talks a lot about our money and our heart attitude toward it. He is much more concerned about our hearts.

The forefathers of our faith had unimaginable wealth. Job owned 7,000 sheep, 3,000 camels, 500 teams of oxen, and 500 female donkeys. He also had many servants and was, in fact, the richest person in the entire land.

We learn that father Abraham was extremely rich in live-stock, silver, and gold (Gen.13:2). We are told that Isaac acquired so many flocks of sheep and goats, herds of cattle, and servants that the Philistines became jealous of him (Gen. 26:14).

Then we can read nearly three pages of how Jacob's wealth grew while his father-in-law's flocks decreased (Gen. 30-31). And finally, we learn that King Solomon became richer and wiser than any other king on earth (1 Kings 10:3). This included his dear old dad, King David.

There were many people in the Bible who were wealthy. And while Jesus spoke much about wealth, when it comes to our own finances, we often remember the story of the rich young man. He was asked by Jesus to take his possessions, sell them, give the money to the poor and come follow Him.

We are petrified that Jesus will ask us to do the same. But let's look more closely at their conversation in Luke 18 to better understand Jesus' response.

One day one of the local officials approached Jesus addressing Him as a "Good Teacher" and asking what he must do to deserve eternal life. This man was focused on "what Jesus did" rather than "Who Jesus was." In an effort to refocus and redirect him, clarifying the young man's spiritual vision Jesus asked:

"Why are you calling Me good?
No one is good—only God."

The rich young ruler needed to recognize Jesus as God–the Highest Ruler. When the conversation continues, Jesus recognizes this man's focus and responds in *Luke 18:18-30 saying:

"'You know the commands,
no illicit sex, no killing, no stealing, no lying,
honor your father and mother.'"

When the ruler retorted that he had kept all the commands for as long as he could remember, Jesus said:

"Then there's only one thing left to do:
Sell everything you own and give it away to the poor.
You will have riches in heaven.
Then come,
follow me.'"

Notice these last two words. The man needed Jesus. He needed a Savior. But he missed the point and left very sad because he was holding onto *the things he wanted* rather than *the One He needed.*

Interestingly, this is the only time Jesus, acting on behalf of God, tells anyone to sell all their riches. Could it be specifically because this man wanted his riches more than he wanted God?

I think Jesus knew that his riches had first place in his heart and that he defined himself more by wealth than anything else. This ruler never recognizes Jesus as anyone more than a "good teacher."

Like my daughter who thought she needed a blue cake with green icing, this young man also confused his wants with his needs. He was not willing to give up his treasures "for a time." Notice that he was not going to lose his riches, but rather by giving them away, he would gain riches in heaven.

So often Jesus spoke in parables, painting a picture by telling a story. This is not a parable but a real person who **hungered for wonder.** This young man was living his real life when he encountered Life Himself.

Since I like stories with happy endings, this is not my favorite story as the rich young man left sorrowful. While he

hungered for wonder, he saw only the temporary loss, rather than the eternal gain. Jesus commented in Matthew 19:24 that:

> "It is easier for a camel to go through a needle's eye,
> than for a rich man to enter into the kingdom of God."

Sounds pretty difficult, doesn't it? But with God all things are possible (Matthew 19:26). The one thing that the wealthy man lacked and truly needed was Jesus–Who saw his lonely heart.

The rich man walked away filled with sorrow yet hungry because he held so tightly to his wealth–not differentiating his wants and his needs, much like my daughter. This causes me to stop to ask myself a few reflective questions.

Do I sometimes hold too tightly to the things of this world? What do I hold to most tightly? As a master carpenter Himself, Jesus hit the nail on the head when He saw this man's heart. Jesus knew his identify was wrapped and warped by his wealth such that he couldn't let go to gain what he needed most.

We remember this rich young ruler by the three things that defined him: his wealth, his age, and his position. What defines you?

I want to be able to differentiate wants from needs trusting God to supply all my needs. Philippians 4:19 promises us:

> "You can be sure that God will take care of everything you need,
> his generosity exceeding even yours in the glory
> that pours from Jesus.

> Our God and Father abounds in glory
> that just pours out into eternity."

God wants to satiate our **hunger for wonder**; He wants to give us more than just blue cake with green icing.

THE JOURNEY FORWARD:

For today's exercise, could you write the first line of Philippians 4:19 (from above) on a slip of paper and place it with the money in your wallet or wrap the slip of paper around the credit card you most commonly use. When you wait in line at a check-out, can you reflect on it and commit it to memory? It might be a good exercise to glance at the items you have chosen to purchase.

- How many of the items in your cart are necessities?
- How many are wants?
- Do you trust God to supply all your needs?
- What are your most important needs?

CORN ON THE COB

*T*oday on our journey as we **hunger for wonder**, I have a question for you that I have been pondering since I cleaned up the dinner table. If given the choice, which would you rather have: a piece of corn on the cob that still had the strings from the husk, or a piece that had no strings but no corn? Are you thinking that's not much of a choice really?

Personally, I'd pass on both, but not my daughter and son. Alyssa delights in finding strings that she can confiscate from her corn on the cob. It's a challenge that her little fingers can't pass up.

My son, on the other hand, loves to suck on the bare cob. Add some butter and he bounces with joy in his highchair. As Garrett struggles to grip on the slippery cob, he grins exposing all four of his pearly whites. He kicks his feet in glee as he giggles and gnaws.

∾

CHILDREN TAKE PLEASURE IN SUCH SIMPLE DELIGHTS. I CAN LEARN a lot from them about my attitude and perspective. Though the English words "attitude" and "perspective" do not appear in the Bible, God's Word has much to say about both our attitude and perspective on life.

Would it surprise you to know that both are choices we make? In our pursuit of **wonder**, I have taken note of my daughter's **wonder**-filled response. She sees strings differently. Strings are challenges.

I have a lot of strings in my life…challenges in my marriage, challenges with my children, challenges with my work and challenges with managing my time. What challenges do you have that are the "stringiest?"

I've decide that any "string" I encounter on my journey for **wonder** is going to remind me of the silky strings on my daughter's corn. I want my attitude to be different based on my perspective that has changed.

Just as my daughter likes strings, my son truly loves his butter-soaked cob. I remember sucking butter from the cob as a kid. Back in the day, Mom bought margarine because she thought it was better for us. Margarine mingled with the juice from the cob tasted…well…corny and yummy. But then I grew up and I became too dignified for such behavior.

Do you ever feel like you miss **wonder** when you forgo the small pleasures in life? I'll admit, sometimes I don't buy corn on the cob because I'm just too busy to deal with the preparation. I grab a bag of corn in the frozen food section and call it good. Eating corn on the cob is too troublesome, I've told myself.

If anyone knew that life could be laden with "strings" of troubling trials, Paul knew firsthand. In Philippians, he explains his attitude toward life saying that he doesn't have a sense of needing anything personally. Paul had learned to be content whatever his circumstances sharing in Philipians 4:3:

"I've found the recipe for being happy
whether full or hungry,
hands full or hands empty.
Whatever I have, wherever I am,
I can make it through anything
in the One who makes me who I am."

To paraphrase loosely, Paul would be happy with corn that had strings or with a cob with no corn at all. It is a matter of perspective; sometimes children have a simple perspective that we have lost and then work years to achieve. In Matthew *18:3-4, Jesus reminds us of that simplicity when He encourages us to:

"Return to square one and start over like children...
Whoever becomes simple and elemental again,
like this child,
will rank high in God's kingdom."

Is it no **wonder** that Jesus enjoyed children? They are innocent. They are humble. They can be content with whatever the state of their cob. Which makes me ask myself if I am content?

When every TV commercial and internet ad is tempting you to want whatever widget they are selling, being satisfied is a challenge. St. James wrote about stringy challenges in *James 1:2-4 telling us to consider it a gift when:

"tests and challenges come at you from all sides."

Then He explains that these trials refine our faith producing endurance. He encourages us saying:

"Don't try to get out of anything prematurely.
Let it do its work so you become mature and well-developed,
not deficient in any way."

This makes me reflect on how I react to the trials that string together my moments into months. Most days I am joyful. Though I do admit that at times I struggle when I take my eyes off my blessings and start looking at everyone else's "cob."

JOURNEY FORWARD:

Might you work corn on the cob into your dinner menu this week or order it when eating out? When enjoying it, could you use it as an opportunity to evaluate your perspective?

MY CHIPPED FRONT TOOTH

*C*an you believe we are halfway through our quest together as we **hunger for wonder?** As I brushed my teeth this morning, I asked God to show me something extra-ordinary in the ordinary. And He did. What could be more ordinary than teeth?

I smiled at my reflection in the mirror and shook my head amazed that God would bring to my mind a picture my Mom had taken at Sears by a professional photographer when I was about eleven.

I specifically remember not wanting to smile because earlier that week I had fallen on the brick patio in my sprint inside to answer a phone call from Kimmy, my cousin. I remember pushing myself up on my bloodied elbows and being horrified to see half of my front tooth lying on the brick. Shrieking, I ran into the house to find my Mom's loving arms.

On the way inside, I must have dropped the other half of my tooth. It was nowhere to be found, although my Dad searched until dusk with his Eveready® flashlight. He didn't know what else to do for his chipped beauty.

My Mom had my friend, Susie Stuckey, come up the alley for supper. She made pizza, my all-time favorite meal, but so much of my tooth was missing, it hurt to bite off the crust. I cried until my eyes were puffy, as I didn't think I was pretty anymore. I was embarrassed to smile.

The Mattoon mayor was also the dentist in town. Dr. Dettro felt he should wait to properly cap my tooth as he said my gums would recede as I matured. So, he fashioned a make-shift cap which wasn't the same shade of white as my other teeth, but it certainly was an improvement. It discolored over time. I remember begging my parents for a real cap before I started high school.

When I turned sixteen, Dr. Dettro felt my gums had receded enough for a permanent cap. I was so grateful to finally have a better front tooth...one that wasn't semi-translucent and was closer to the actual color of my other teeth.

Back then, caps were metal covered with porcelain, so the one thing about the cap that was still conspicuous was the underlying metal rim around my gum line. In some pictures, I remember critiquing my teeth and reminding myself not to smile so big which allowed the metal to be more obvious. As time passed, my gums receded more, and the silver underlay was even more noticeable.

~

NOW YEARS LATER, PEOPLE COMPLIMENT ME ON MY SMILE SAYING it's one of my best features. Funny how God can take what we think is marred and make it a **wonderful**. Have you experienced this personally? If so, this is your testimony. Others may benefit from hearing it.

God can take our upside moments (when we quite literally slip and fall landing face down on a brick) and turn them right side up creating a **W.O.W.** moment. He can take the bad and make it better. He can embrace what we think is an imperfection or weakness and transform it into a strength. He sees our beauty and reminds us in * 2 Corinthians 12:9:

> "My grace is enough;
> it's all you need.
> My strength comes into its own in your weakness."

This seems to be a paradox. It defies human understanding and reasoning, but it is a principle of His kingdom, like the law of gravity is a principle of this earth. You and I can rely on gravity to keep us from floating away just as we can rely on His grace to cover our imperfections. Saint Paul did when He wrote the above verse.

Did you know that Paul was given grace instead of what he had asked for? Much like my chipped tooth, Paul had an imperfection or "thorn" that he prayed would be taken away? He wanted to be restored.

I can sure relate. More than anything the day I chipped half of my front tooth off, I wanted it restored. But in Paul's case, God left the "thorn." And Paul tells us specifically why God did in verse 7. Paul admits that God allowed the "thorn to keep him humble" because God didn't want him becoming "puffed up."

God knew Paul, inside and out. He saw something in Paul that could benefit from the thorn. This is difficult to read and hear because we can't always see what God sees. We don't always understand His ways, that are more complete than our understanding (Isaiah 55:8).

Like Saint Paul, do you have something that you have asked to be restored, but God has not answered yet in a way that you fully grasp? I certainly don't understand why God restores in some cases and why He allows thorns to remain in others.

There have been areas of my life, where God has not removed the thorn or burden. In those areas, if I am honest with you, I have struggled. Some days have been better than others. But even in the hardest days, God has provided an abiding joy... an undergirding joy...and a profound joy.

I am happy.

I am filled.

I am fulfilled.

And I radiate joy...often in my smile.

Which brings me back to my teeth. I have frequently thought about how very different my smile would be if I were born even 100 years earlier when caps for teeth did not exist. Just the thought of a chipped tooth keeps me humble. It makes me ever so thankful that I have a cap every day when I brush and floss.

Likewise, it seems Paul was humble in how he responded to the remaining "thorn." After that Paul stopped focusing on the handicap and began appreciating it as a gift. He tells us that he started accepting the limitations in stride, and with a good attitude.

He found that when he allowed Christ to take over the weaker he got physically, the stronger he became spiritually. So Paul's response to his thorn changed even though God's response never changed. And therein lies the **wonder.**

God changed Paul's heart toward his circumstances. God showed Paul the "gift" rather than changing his circumstances. What circumstances do you have today that you would like God to change? I don't know what His answer will be, but I do know that He will listen.

As with Saint Paul, He may not change your circumstances. But He may answer your prayer, like He did mine in restoring my tooth through Dr. Dettro. I understand that to many people a cap may seem simply like a dental advance, but to me, it was an answer to prayer. I thank God when He answers my prayers, even when he works through other people, like a dentist, a doctor or a pharmacist.

When I was eleven, He provided me with inner happiness that was evident in my big smile. The fact that I had a tooth that was imperfect became inconsequential over time.

Today He is still providing. When I think I am too exhausted to smile, He brings me a **W.O.W.** moment that reminds me of His **wonder.** I have come to understand that His grace–His gift–is sufficient for me.

JOURNEY FORWARD:

God is faithful. As I lay sobbing in my bed, He heard a young girl's prayer to be pretty. This is my testimony. Has God restored something for you? If so, smile and thank Him. Might you be willing to share your testimony when asked?

GERBER'S STRAINED PEAS

They look disgusting. They taste disgusting. They smell disgusting. They feel disgusting. They even leave disgusting stains. But my little six-month-old, thinks they are de-e-e-e-e-licious!

They are his favorite food. In fact, he recognizes the color of the jar when I reach for it in the cabinet and starts clapping his hands and kicking his feet so hard his highchair rocks.

What you ask? Gerber's strained peas. His fondness of peas has become our source of **wonder** today. You would think I had a jar of Smuckers® fudge topping. His sister likes to watch him enjoy his feast. Out of excitement he drools the peas down his chin. He is so caught up in the joy of the moment, he blows strained pea bubbles. Anyone within two feet should be dressed in plastic.

~

MY DAUGHTER WANTS TO FEED HIM PEAS FOR EVERY MEAL AND SHE never lets me forget to pick up peas at the store. In fact, it has become her job to count the jars of peas as she loads them in the shopping cart.

Thirteen is as high as she can count; probably a good thing, thirteen jars of peas a week may just be his limit. After all, he barely weighs twice that in pounds. While I **hunger for wonder,** I could eat fudge topping from a jar and forego the strained peas. How about you?

From my son's perspective, strained peas are **wonderfully** scrumptious. No salt. No butter. Just room temperature smashed peas with a touch of water added for easy swallowing. We gag at the thought. Our taste buds have grown up and our palates are more refined. Our thoughts on what we like have changed based on our experiences of tastier foods.

In that manner, strained peas are much like our life here on earth. Let me explain. From our vantage point here on the third planet from the sun, we think in three dimensions. We are limited in our ability to understand what life in heaven will be like. We wake up every morning, trudge our way through our day.

At night we say our prayers, kiss our kids, say *sleep well* to our spouse, close our eyes, and snooze. We are confined to thinking about heaven in terms of the days we have experienced here on earth. How many times have you said, "There just aren't enough hours in a day?"

Think about it. In heaven we will have eternal days. There will be no darkness because the Light of all Lights will be there perpetually. Will that mean that we will never sleep?

Here on earth, we sleep one third of our life, which for most people is over twenty-five years. Will our resurrected bodies need rest, or will we be too busy to snooze? The insight we have on spiritual beings is given to us mostly in descriptions of angels in the Bible. Will we be like the angels, and have assignments? I think so.

There are warrior angels (Ex. 23) and guardian angels (Matt. 18) and messenger angels (Luke 1) and ushering angels (Matt. 25). These are just a few of the jobs angels perform. If we have jobs like the angels do, I would like to meet and greet folks at the pearly gates. Count me in for the Welcome Team. Wouldn't it be awesome to usher believers into God's presence? Hospitality is coded in my DNA by God Himself.

Here on Earth we have seasons, but in heaven it will always be like spring. There will be fruit each of the twelve months of the year on the Trees of Life that border the river that flows from the throne of God (Revelation 22).

If it will always be harvest time, I sense there will be a need for harvesters. My dear friend Christa Lane absolutely loves to garden. She describes the feel of earth between her fingers with such a huge smile. Coming from a small farming community in Illinois, I know lots of farmers who would make great harvesters.

One common question that comes up with some frequency at the Wilt household, since we have two dogs (Betsi and

CoCo) and a cat (Truffles) is "Will doggies and kitties be in heaven?"

We know that when Christ returns, the wolf and the lamb will live together; the leopard will lie down with the baby goat while the calf and yearling will be safe with the lion (Isa.10). Several times in the book of Revelation, Saint John speaks of horses.

Because of these Scripture references, I absolutely do think there will be animals in heaven. Those who are much more educated in Theology than me–who spent a life-time writing about God like C.S. Lewis–seem to agree.

I love that Jesus shares a bit of His Father's perspective on heaven telling us that people will come from every corner of the earth to take their seats of honor. We will be surprised because heaven's order will be very different from earth's order as we learn in Luke 13:29-30:

> "Some who seem least important now
> will be the greatest then,
> and some who are the greatest now
> will be least important then."

There are going to be a lot of surprises when we are finally in heaven. Here on Earth we have what I call "The Strained Pea Mentality" as we strain to see what God has prepared for us. When we try to peek through God's **Window of Wonder** directly into heaven, we struggle because we have nothing that compares.

GERBER'S STRAINED PEAS | 111

We are much like my son, who has never had fudge topping, and doesn't know what he is missing. When I am weary from chores, laden with laundry, wading through worrisome work weeks, encountering impatient patients, heavy traffic, stop lights and stalled cars, I'm going to refocus on the promises, the rewards, the crowns, the comforts, the joy, and the peace that awaits me.

You and I can't begin to fathom the beauty of our Father's mansions from our current address. Even our wildest expectation will fall far short of heaven's wonderful reality. Based on Scripture, I just know that we will be totally awed when we actually arrive.

Truly, that day will be the fulfillment of our **hunger for wonder**, seeing our Savior and His Father face to face. It will be the biggest family reunion ever.

JOURNEY FORWARD:

While my infant son loves strained peas straight out of the jar, my toddler daughter loves green beans straight out of the can. One of her many nick names is "bean," because she loves them so.

What was your favorite food as a child? Mine was orange macaroni and cheese prepared from the blue box. My tastes have changed since childhood, providing me with perspective of how my "tastes" will change when I experience the perfect **wonders** of heaven.

Whatever your favorite food, I suspect that none will taste as perfect as what we experience in heaven. Today as you journey forward, can you enjoy a food you love and let it remind you that the most scrumptious stuff is yet to come?

A CUFFLINK

he hunt was on. It was a frenzied hunt. One that bordered on panic. Frustration reverberated in my husband's voice as he reasoned, "It was just here a minute ago."

Dave was in his tuxedo crawling on his knees looking for his one missing cufflink. I was frantically shoving hair pins in my French roll, trying not to smudge my damp nail polish.

Once every two years the hospital has a ball to raise money for those in need who can't pay their medical bills. Tonight was the night, and we were pressed for time. Minutes earlier my daughter was scampering around our bedroom in her Beauty and the Beast sleeper.

Alyssa was so excited to have Lindsey, her "all growed up friend" in the neighborhood, come to babysit. As she clasped her "monies for pissa" in her little fist, she glowed with the anticipation of having the pizza man come to her very own front door.

She thought it was quite an honor as it was a rare occurrence at our house. It was hard to say which she liked better, paying for the pizza or eating it.

Now she was tugging on my gown with one hand, holding her sippy cup in the other. In a muddled little voice, she rattled off something she deemed important. She was distressed; I was impatient.

"Caught, Mommy," she explained.

I countered, "Mommy doesn't have time now, sweetie." She whimpered and pulled at her ear. It was then that I leaned over and discovered my husband's other cufflink. Yes. She had wedged it in her ear. Was I surprised? Nope.

As the mother of a toddler, I have come to expect the unexpected. As a sojourner who has asked God to help me find **wonder** daily, I am also coming to expect the unexpected. I pray you are too!

DAVE RETRIEVED HIS CUFFLINK WITH MY EYEBROW TWEEZERS AND Alyssa was on her merry way...we were as well. As we drove the twenty minutes into the city, I was left with time to reflect. Thinking of the cufflink embedded in Alyssa's ear, a phrase came to mind that Jesus first said in Matthew 7:13:

"Anyone with ears to hear should listen and understand!"

This phrase appears seven more times in the Gospels (Matt.

7:13, 11:15, 13:9, Mark 4:9, 13:9, 13:23, Luke 14:35) and again seven additional times in the book of Revelation (Rev. 2:7, 2:11, 2:17, 2:29, 3:6, 3:13, 3:22). Could listening be linked to **wonder?**

I remembered, Mrs. Beasley, my 1st grade teacher who was young and pretty. She was the first person who I recall asking me to "Put on my listening ears." Did you have a teacher or parent that said something similar?

My mom used to remind my siblings and me that God created us with one mouth, two eyes and two ears for a reason. Of course, the implication was that seeing and hearing where doubly important.

When we were talking, we didn't learn anything, and my mother always placed value on listening and learning. We can hear her wisdom in *Proverbs 20:12:

> "Ears that hear and eyes that see—
> we get our basic equipment from God!"

Do you find it interesting that Solomon says nothing about the mouth? Our mouth is "basic equipment" too, and yet the Bible's books of wisdom focus on those senses and skills that can help us grow in wisdom and understanding.

In the Bible, the word "listen" is found 331 times and "hear" is found 347 times. As you might suspect, the books of wisdom contain many of these passages. We are told by Solomon–who was known for his wisdom above all else–in Proverbs 8:34:

> "Joyful are those who listen to me."

Listening to God results in joyfulness. Could you use more joy? I'm up for it. Count me in. When Jesus asks us to listen and hear I think He is encouraging us to hear beyond the words. Might He be inviting us to hear deeper spiritual truths?

He wants us to use our ears to hear with our heart. There is a progression...it starts with an **ear** and progresses so that we **hear** with our **heart**. Did you notice the word **ear** hidden within these other words? We each have ears and Jesus always starts with what we have. He does not ask us to do something that He did not equip us to do.

He asks us to give Him our ordinary **ear**s to **hear** extraordinary truths to transform our **heart**. This is when the ordinary h**ear**ing becomes extra-ordinary understanding.

Jesus is asking us to cl**ear** out our **ear**s and draw n**ear** to Him (James 4:8). He invites us to l**ear**n from Him (Matt. 11:29). If we s**ear**ch for Him, we will find Him n**ear** (Matt. 7:7). If we re**ear**range our priorities and place Him first and y**earn** for Truth, He will app**ear** (Matt. 7:8).

With His perfect love, fear will disapp**ear** (1 John 4:18). When we are w**ear**y, He will help b**ear** our burdens (Matt. 11:28). He wants to wipe every t**ear** from our eyes (Rev. 21:4).

Your salvation is worth more than any p**ear**l (Matt. 13:44). It is not something you **earn** (Eph. 2:8). He came to **Ear**th to die for us. You and I are d**ear** to Him (John 3:16).

This y**ear**, this moment, and forever...He wants to be our Savior (2 Pet. 3:9). Do you hear echoes of His grace and love? Perhaps this is why He gave us two ears, so we could hear all His promises. Scripture has always placed a premium on hearing God's voice.

As we learned early on our journey of **wonder** The Shema—one of the two prayers specifically commanded by God through Moses—begins with the phrase from ** Deuteronomy 6:4:

"**Hear** O Israel:
The LORD our God is one LORD."

The Shema is the oldest ancient prayer that is recited every morning and night by faithful Jews around the world. How do you begin and end your day? Do you h**ear**?

JOURNEY FORWARD:

Though you may not have a cuff link embedded in your ear like my daughter, on your journey forward today could you ladies put on your longest pair of dangling earrings?

As you feel them sway and swing throughout the day, can it serve as a reminder to h**ear** with both your **ear**s and your h**ear**t? Guys, when you see a lady w**ear**ing earrings today, let them remind you to h**ear**.

THE TENDERIZER

*N*o doubt about it. Dads are special. As I watch my husband tuck our three-year-old daughter in bed, I am reminded of those nostalgic bedtime moments when I was a kid. Bedtime with my Dad was fun-time.

After he pulled the covers up to our chins and gave us a kiss, Kathy, Brian and I could choose one of two tucks—a tenderizer, or a steamroller. Each was sure to keep us tucked under those covers for the night.

Our least favorite tuck was the steamroller. As Dad said, "Only the tough and the rough order the steamroller." He would lie down on the bed beside us and roll right over us. A steamroller deserved its name as it flattened everyone in its path. Of course, Mom had more than two cents to say about that tuck.

We all favored "the tenderizer." Dad could tenderize better

than anyone else. He used the sides of his hands to "karate chop" us faster than a drum roll from head to toe and back again. The tenderizer seemed to vibrate every last giggle from our tired little bodies.

TWENTY-FIVE YEARS AGO, I THOUGHT THAT NO ONE COULD TOP my Dad at "tenderizing." I now understand that God is the best "Tenderizer" in the business. He is the only one that can touch a human's hardened heart.

As Christians, He lives in us. His Spirit can work on our inner being, if we will allow Him to have control. As we journey together in search of **wonder**, who controls our hearts?

By walking close to Him, we can better understand Paul's advice in **Hebrews 3:12 to be cautious, guarding our hearts so that they don't become:

"hardened through the deceitfulness of sin."

Without Christ, our hearts are inherently prone to wander toward evil. Even though we may be Christian, as Paul explained to the Hebrews, our hearts can be hardened by sin.

Most of us do not purposefully seek to harden our hearts, but if we allow sin to remain unchecked in our lives, we are at risk for hardened hearts.

A hardened heart lacks innocence.

A hardened heart is less pliable to others.

A hardened heart is resistant to change.

A hardened heart is less likely to be opened toward others. Those with hardened hearts can lack soft responses. Hearts that wander far from our Father, lack a sense of His **wonder**. Hardened hearts can cause pain both for ourselves and others.

Calcified hearts can be more challenging than any heart disease that a cardiologist might diagnose and treat. Do we realize what consequences our sins carry? Saint Paul did. This is why he warned us about the consequences of sin.

Paul wants us to have hearts that are soft and open to God and others. Hearts that experience **wonder** and love like innocent children. How do we keep our hearts innocent and young?

Based on Scripture, giving our hearts to Christ to be "born again" seeking Him daily is one way. Avoiding sin is another based on Paul's admonishments to in *Hebrews 3:8,10:

"Don't harden your hearts as Israel did when they rebelled,
when they tested me in the wilderness...
So, I was angry with them, and I said,
'Their hearts always turn away from me.
They refuse to do what I tell them.'"

These words are meant for us as well. Wouldn't you agree that avoiding sin is much easier said than done? Sometimes we seem caught in sin's vicious cycle. Why? The answer lies in our hearts.

Sin begins in the heart. God wants us to turn to Him and accept Christ into our hearts as both Savior and Lord. He can "tenderize" the hardest of hearts. In Ezekiel 36:26a our Father promises:

> "And I will give you a new heart,
> and I will put a new spirit in you.
> I will take out your stony, stubborn heart
> and give you a **tender**, responsive heart."

If you know someone that seems hardened and unapproachable, Christ can work miracles in their heart. I've seen it happen in my own family.

If you know someone that is so entrenched in a life of sin that they seem immovable, Christ can move them to contrition. Again, I am a witness to these miracles.

If you know someone that seems so determined to avoid attending church, Christ can speak to them in the silence of their very heart. He has mastered the art of "tenderizing."

THE JOURNEY FORWARD:

Before you tuck yourself in bed tonight, can you pray for someone who needs Christ to soften their heart? Sometimes it's easier to see needs in others but might there be an area of your heart that needs to be more tender toward someone?

On our journey forward, can we together do our best to live out **Ephesians 4:32:

"Be ye kind one to another,
tenderhearted,
forgiving one another, even as God for Christ's sake hath
forgiven you."

THE BALLOON

*T*hey come in all colors, shapes and sizes. Some are as large as the Good Year Blimp while others are as small as your fist. Some are metallic while most are latex. Some have helium. But most have 21% oxygen, 78% nitrogen, and 1% carbon dioxide, carbon monoxide and nitrous oxide which is just plain air. Yet they all have one thing in common; balloons bring **wonder** to children.

It is nearly Easter, and my daughter still has her metallic heart balloon from Valentine's Day tied to the handlebars of her tricycle. It glides behind her like a friend waiting to be noticed. The faster she peddles, the more merrily it meanders about the ceiling. It bobs back and forth as she rides round and round the pool table in our basement. My son is enthralled; his gleaming eyes are glued.

~

As I watched my son filled with wonder, I had a W.O.W. moment and it struck me that a balloon filled with air has a story to tell. Air ordinarily is not something we "see." But when it fills a balloon bringing it to life, we suddenly notice air.

Air has much in common with faith. Faith is not something we can ordinarily "see." But when a person of faith shows extraordinary kindness, suddenly their faith become visible, much like air that suddenly fills a balloon.

Saint James asks what good faith is if others don't see our faith by how we live. He purposes that an inactive faith is an invalid faith. Practically speaking he asks what good faith is if we see fellow neighbors in need of food or clothing and we do nothing more than wish them a good day.

He feels strongly that our faith needs to be life-changing both for us and for those around us insisting in James 2:17-18 that:

"Faith by itself isn't enough.
Unless it produces good deeds,
it is dead and useless.
Now someone may argue,
'Some people have faith;
others have good deeds.'
But I say,
'How can you show me your faith
if you don't have good deeds?

I will show you my faith by my good deeds.'"

So, what I hear James saying is that faith becomes evident and visible to others by our good works done in Jesus' name. Which is exactly the story my daughter's heart shaped balloon is telling me through the air visible inside the balloon.

Balloons can bring others joy. I pray that my faith when shared lovingly through kind deeds will bring others joy as well. Christ gives us joy because He loves us and wants us to share that joy with others.

While good deeds bring joy to others, good deeds along with the Good News of salvation can bring greater joy...eternal joy through saving faith in Christ. This brings to focus another similarity between faith and air.

Just as air is essential to our physical life, faith is essential to our spiritual life (Ephesians 2:8). Some days I feel filled with faith. Other days I feel a bit deflated like a balloon left over from a celebration that was weeks earlier.

Do you ever feel deflated? Times when you need to be encouraged and re-inflated by having your faith reaffirmed? In those times, I turn to God through Scripture. We are told by Paul in Romans 10:17 how to gain and expand our faith:

"So faith comes from hearing,
that is, hearing the Good News about Christ."

It sounds as simple and as straight-forward as blowing up a

balloon. Does it ring with familiarity from yesterday's devotion about hearing?

There are many ways to hear God. We can hear when others reach out to us through kind deeds done in Christ's name. We can hear as we read aloud or hear God through His Word as we read in silence.

We can hear as we listen to our pastor's sermon, our parents, our teachers, our mentors, and our friends. We can hear as we listen to Christian radio programming and hear the lyrics on the songs. We can hear our Creator in creation all around us (Romans 1:20).

I'm sure there are many more ways to hear God. How do you hear Him most clearly? Does hearing God encourage and fill you?

JOURNEY FORWARD:

On today's journey can you to take a few moments to reflect... are you hearing the Word of God and letting Him fill you? When you hear God, are you more open to seeing His **wonder**? Is your faith made visible by your good deeds–like air is made visible by a balloon–and is there a good deed that you could do for someone today in Christ's name?

SHOW AND TELL

$\mathcal{D}$o you remember the **wonder** and anticipation of Show and Tell? The exhilaration of having a particularly special item to show your peers and even the disappointment of forgetting something you could share and being the only kid with nothing exciting to present?

I remember all those feelings that have been pinned and pasted from grade school very neatly on my mind's bulletin board. And today, on our search to satiate our **hunger for wonder**, we are returning to the art of Show and Tell.

So many years ago, as students we were called upon to Show and Tell. As Christians, could we also be called upon to Show and Tell? In the last devotional, we learned that people can see and experience our invisible faith, when they see and experience our visible deeds much like invisible air becomes visible in a balloon.

While we "show" others our faith through our generosity and kindness, is there a message that we could also "tell" them? When I look at the consistent example of Jesus throughout His ministry, He not only met people's physical needs, He met their deeper spiritual needs. Sometimes they hadn't even identified these needs.

As we **hunger for wonder** today let's go directly to The Source. When we turn to John 6:26-35 we read that Jesus understood that people came to Him for a free lunch...quite literally. He *fed people* and *freed people* healing them. He understood it was about *what He gave* not *who He was*. And He corrected and redirected people saying:

"Don't be so concerned about perishable things like food. Spend your energy seeking eternal life."

Then Jesus made a monumental statement declaring:

"I am the bread of life. Whoever comes to me will never be hungry again."

To me, meeting people's physical needs seems easier than meeting their spiritual needs. I can share a meal from my crock pot. But I can't always understand what they are experiencing and tell them what to expect if I haven't walked through that valley before.

The reality is we cannot fully meet their spiritual needs, only God can. We may not know what they most need. They might not even know what they most need, but God does.

Can we introduce them to Christ? I'll be transparent with you. I have struggled with this not wanting to be too pushy and not knowing how people may react.

Oftentimes, when I reach out to someone in need I just say, "God bless you." Sometimes I add, "Please, know that God loves you." But can I do more? Can I share the Good News bottled for those who thirst? It's one line from John 3:16:

> "For this is how God loved the world:
> He gave his one and only Son,
> so that everyone who believes in him will not perish
> but have eternal life."

I find that I sometimes make things more complex than they need to be. In kindergarten we learned how to Show and Tell and maybe I just need to get back to the basics. When I hand someone a bottle of water and a granola bar, maybe I could also share in my own words the truth of John 3:16:

God loves you and it is in His name that I am called to share that love. Please know that He sent His Son to die for **our** sins so that **anyone** who believes in Him will not die but will live forever with Him in heaven.

That's two sentences and that "tells" the Good News. Surely, I can do that. I may have to practice a few times to feel comfortable, but if in kindergarten I could share during Show and Tell, I can do it now. Right? So, there you have it - the Biblical art of Show and Tell.

Though it may have been years since you were chosen to stand before your peers for Show and Tell, know that you are chosen by God to Show and Tell as long ago established in *1 Peter 2:9-10 which says:

"But you are the ones chosen by God...
to do his work and speak out for him,
to **tell** others of the night-and-day difference he made for you—
from nothing to something,
from rejected to accepted."

JOURNEY FORWARD:

On your journey forward today, can you **show** someone your love for God with a kind deed and **tell** them about your Savior?

GOOD AND ICKY

*I*t was the first snow of the season and my daughter–like kids across the nation–wanted to go outside to play and sample the manna colored delicacy. Since the sun was barely up, I asked her to wait a few "Scooby Doos," which is how we measure the passage of time.

With the sun barely bouncing above the horizon, I gave in. We bundled up though the temperature hadn't warmed up. Her first step onto the snow-covered step reminded me of the **W.O.W.** moment when astronaut Neal Armstrong declared:

"That's one small step for man,
one giant leap for mankind."

My daughter crunched cautiously down the stairs with the same **wonder.** Then she did what just comes natural for kids.

She scooped up a big mitten of snow and into her mouth it went.

Next, we were on a mission. Every square foot of our yard had to have her footprint signature before we could come in. Heaven forbid, the snow stayed smooth and unscathed.

Later that afternoon we headed to the grocery store and, once again, she had to sample the snow. This snow, however, was right outside the automatic doors. Carts had been pushed through it for hours as folks had stomped in the slush. But to a small child snow is edible, despite dirt content. As you can guess, it went into her mouth before I could get "NO" out of my mouth.

As I wiped the grunge off her mittens and chin, I attempted to explain the difference between good and icky snow. Although she didn't grasp the essence of germs, she did understand that good snow doesn't taste and feel like sand. As shopping carts sledged past, like Moses, I laid down the law:

"Thou shall not eat icky snow."

Okay, so while I certainly didn't resemble Charlton Heston in the 1956 hugely successful Biblical Epic of *The Ten Commandments,* I had her best interests at heart when it came to snow eating.

My command was issued out of love. She **hungered for the wonder** of clean snow. Gritty snow left her disenchanted, trying to spit the grit. As I cleaned her tongue with my scarf, I was reminded of God's commands to us.

Once we were home and the groceries were safely stowed, Alyssa colored. I opened my Bible to Exodus 20:1-17, where God shares His Ten Commandments.

The first three provide the foundational framework for our relationship with Him while the last seven build on that foundation for our relationship with others. When you think of these Ten Commandments, what feeling comes to mind?

Do you feel grateful that God provides these rules so that we know our boundaries and so that society has a moral framework? Or do you feel like God wants to control you, to deny you pleasures, to thwart your happiness?

The feelings you have might be a reflection of how you perceive God based on your relationship with your parents. As a parent now myself, I have a caregiver's perspective based on rules I give my children to safeguard them from potential harm.

His laws give us a standard by which we can compare good and evil. It allows us to see the sin innate to our nature. In this way the law laid the groundwork, if you would, for the need for the coming of Jesus. The first step in salvation is recognizing that we have sinned and fallen short of God's glory which leads to the next step; the realization of the need for a Savior.

Today, as much as the day Moses walked down from Mount Sinai with the stone tablets held high over his head, The Ten Commandments deserve our attention. But try as I might, I can't keep every command flawlessly. This is why I am so grateful for God's grace.

God wants you and me to experience the **wonder** of His world covered in sparkling snow. Which brings me back to His grace. King David never met Jesus, but He understood the need for grace when He wrote in Psalm 51:7:

> "Purify me from my sins,
> and I will be clean;
> wash me,
> and I will be whiter than snow."

This passage points us to Christ and His grace. A few hundred years after the reign of King David, and nearly 700 years before Jesus was born, Isaiah prophesied about our Savior saying in Isaiah 1:18:

> "Though your sins are like scarlet,
> I will make them as white as snow."

While I don't know if you live in an area where you have snow, I do know from these passages that snow can provide a **Window of Wonder** reminding us of the **wonder** of Christ's covering our icky sin with a blanket of good snow.

Snow is an example of Romans 1:20 in action where learn that we can come to know our Creator through His creation. Nature shows us His divine nature. Snow shows us God's grace. He provided Jesus as our Savior to cover our sins making us as pure as fresh snow.

THE JOURNEY FORWARD:

Because you may not have snow, fill a glass completely with ice. After the ice melts, notice that the glass is no longer completely filled. This serves as a lesson on our journey forward. Like ice is hard, keeping God's Law is hard; it will never totally fill us, as melted ice never totally fills the glass.

Just as the ice will melt, we will fall short of keeping His commands. The law points us toward Christ's grace. In Him, we are completely filled.

BARBECUE POTATO CHIPS

 vividly remember the day I ate my first barbecue potato chip. In complete honesty, I should rephrase that as I didn't eat just one chip but rather one whole bag...and it wasn't my bag but rather my best friend and next-door neighbor's, Lori. Odd what landmarks of childhood form lasting memories. The scene is forever inked in my mind.

It was a crisp spring day, and the sun was shining. Lori had gone into her house to find a snack and had emerged with an orangey red sack that had a barbecue grill on the front. Since then, I have come to recognize the brand as Lay's chips.

Although we rarely had junk food at our house, I had eaten chips, but I had never had BBQ flavor. Lori said they were spicy. While I didn't think I would like something hot, my hunger persuaded me to give one a try.

We were sitting on the door step of her front porch. I stayed on that step until the entire bag was gone. My taste buds were in love. Twenty-five years later, that same front step on the house remains...as does my love of barbecue chips.

THESE DAYS HOWEVER, I KNOW THAT AN ENTIRE BAG IS unhealthy, so I limit my indulgence. Resisting the urge to overindulge on our favorite foods is tough.

The flesh can be difficult to bring under control. Appetites for food, romance, beauty, excitement and money can hurl perpetual temptations.

Though St. Paul surely never sat on the front step to his tent polishing off a bag of barbecue chips, he struggled with the appetite of his flesh as well.

In frustration, he writes about his internal battle telling us that he desperately needs help. He knows the law, yet he struggles to obey the law, realizing that he doesn't have the willpower.

He shares that his sinful flesh keeps sabotaging him. He "wills" it, but he can't do it. He wants to "do" good, but He can't "be" good. He doesn't want to be bad, but he is bad. He shares in frustration that his decisions don't result in actions.

And he concludes that something has gone wrong deep within him because he falls flat on his face and fails. In fact, he says he disappoints himself so often that it is predictable. He feels like an utter failure in the war against his flesh. Sin gets the

better of him even though he truly delights in God's commandments. In desperation he shares *Romans 7:24:

"I'm at the end of my rope.
Is there no one who can do anything for me?"

Hmm. He sounds pretty down to earth and relatable for a
saint. And sometimes you and I feel like we are the only ones
that are unsuccessful in taming our appetites and are at the end
of our rope.

We know Paul as a man of monumental faith. He suffered
more persecutions than the pages in this book. He converted
countless numbers of the first Christians, authored fourteen epis-
tles comprising most of our New Testament and died for his faith.

The scope of his ministry is probably only surpassed by Jesus
Himself. So, his imperfect example comforts me to know that
even the holiest of humans still struggled.

Like Paul, when we Christians talk about the "battle of the
flesh," we are referring to those opposing forces at work
between knowing what we should do and then doing it. The
flesh and our spirit are in opposition.

I picture this spiritual struggle as a teeter-totter, like the one
my dad built for us when I was a kid. If my big sister was down,
I was up in the air. The same is true in the struggle with the
flesh. When one is in control, the other is out of control, that's
why we struggle with "ups and downs."

While I still occasionally slip up and chow down on too

many chips, I have learned to satisfy myself with good things. So instead of sitting down with a whole big bag, I buy a one serving size bag and then eat a full cup of dip. Yes. You read that right. I eat an entire cup of dip!

I make it from a large carton of cottage cheese that I have blended with my emulsion wand to the same creamy consistency as sour cream. Then I add a package of ranch dip or French onion soup mix.

If you don't have a wand mixer, you can use a blender. It's a guilt free way to enjoy as much healthy dip as I want, while minimizing the unhealthy chips. When my tiny bag is empty, if I want more, I grab a bag of baby carrots. It's hard to eat an entire bag of carrots, but no harm if I do.

While this is a solution I have found that works for me regarding my love of barbecue potato chips, is there a solution that you might find–with the Holy Spirit's help–that could help you in a specific "battle with your flesh?"

Jesus told His disciples straight up in Matthew 26:41:

"The spirit indeed is willing,
but the flesh is weak."

He spoke these words the night before His death when He desperately needed company; He asked His disciples to stay with Him. He was afraid to be crucified. His disciples loved Him; their spirits were willing, but their flesh was weary. I can sure relate.

THE JOURNEY FORWARD:

What battle of the flesh do you struggle with most? Name it. There is power in the written word. Write it down in the blanks below asking God to help lead you not into the temptation of _____ and to deliver you from _____. God is in the delivering business. Moreover, He is in the redeeming business.

KISSES FOR BABY JESUS

*I*t's Christmastime. The house is decorated, and my daughter is thoroughly enjoying all the "pretties," most of which have moved down in rank from "untouchables" to "okay to touch but just be careful" items. She loves stringing pearl garland on the lower branches of the tree, then on her, and then on the tree again. God is providing **W.O.W.** moments strung throughout my day as I enjoy seeing her delight in the season. It is a precious sight.

But perhaps the decorations that intrigue her most are snow globes. Ours has the manger scene inside and plays music. Of course, the first night she noticed it perched high out of her reach she asked "What's dat?"

My husband took it down to show it to her. She squealed as the snow whirled around the baby's manger and quickly informed us, "Dat's baby Jesus stuck in there. And His Mommy and His Daddy to-o-o-o-o-o-o!"

Today we were out for a walk with snow crunching beneath our feet and happened upon a life size plastic manger scene in our neighborhood. You would have thought Alyssa was Christopher Columbus pointing out land. She stopped still in her tracks.

"Look Mommy dat's BABY JESUS!" Then with her big girl snow boots, she bounded across our neighbor's lawn, up to the porch, and toward the plastic figures. My first inclination was to holler for her to stop. But, it was too late and what harm would she cause?

Little did I know she would pick up the plastic baby and rock Him in her arms, giving Him hugs and kisses. Next a hug and kiss for Mary and then Joseph who she adoringly calls "JoeJoe." She was filled with **wonder.**

I STOOD ON THE SIDEWALK WONDERING IF THE HOMEOWNERS SAW her near their porch. Initially I was half embarrassed, then I remembered Jesus' own words when He said in Matthew 19:14:

"Let the children come to me.
Don't stop them!
For the Kingdom of Heaven belongs to those
who are like these children."

Christ had so many people pulling on Him, tugging Him their direction and vying for His attention. Having two under the age of three, I know how draining kids can be. Surely, He was tired.

He wanted to help and heal, to save and protect. Yet He knew He had to deal with the physical limitations that being human placed on Him as He set aside His omnipresence.

I still struggle to imagine the Creator of the universe being trapped in a physical body. Before Jesus came to Earth, He was omnipresent. Now, He was in just one place and forced to walk to travel to another.

No cars.

No jumbo jets.

Just an occasional donkey for transportation. Imagine the overwhelming responsibility He felt. The sorrow. The shortest verse in the Bible, John 11:35, tells us:

"Jesus wept."

It encapsulates His humanness. Isaiah describes Him in Isaiah 53:3 as a:

"Man of sorrows."

Even though He was limited physically by His human body, being both man and God, His divine nature still maintained His omniscience.

He knew everything (John 16:30).

He read every thought (Mark 2:8).

He knew the future of those around Him (John 21:19).

He knew His future (Mark 8:31).

He knew He faced a grueling death (Matthew 16:21).

He knew His dearest friends would be killed (Mark 8:34).

Some would be crucified upside down (John 13:37).

Some would be stoned (Acts 7:58).

Many beaten (Acts 4,5,6).

Jesus lived daily with the oppression of the consequences of sin. He saw disease. He experienced death. And He knew that the human body was created to enjoy health and eternal life, had humankind not chosen to rebel.

The frustration He felt must have been enormous. We live with frustrations daily. Can you relate in some sense? Jesus put His whole heart into His ministry. He left no one group out.

The Gentiles and the Jews.

The sick and healthy.

The sinners and the saints.

The poor and the rich.

The old and the young. Yet children held a special place in Jesus' heart. Perhaps it was because they are innocent and blameless–an oasis of innocence in an ocean of evil. Jesus would be pleased that my daughter wanted to greet Him enthusiastically with a kiss and a hug.

THE JOURNEY FORWARD:

Rather than the routine of reading, just take a few silent moments in awe before God. Notice Him, when the snows of this life are swirling, and you feel trapped like a plastic figure in a snow globe. Greet Him like toddlers greet snow and Christmas decorations. Praise Him. Thank Him. Adore Him.

UP AND DOWN AND AROUND

hen I was a kid, we had the best backyard on the block. In fact, we even had more things to play on than Washington Park, one block north of our home. The feature attraction was the teeter totter that went up and down and even twirled around. My Dad made it along with everything else.

My personal favorite was the playhouse. He put a little sink in it and connected a garden hose to the outside, so we would have running water. The Plexiglas® windows opened and closed.

We even had a miniature replica of a Maytag washing machine inside. And best of all, it was so pretty. "Just like my pretty girls," my dad would say.

When Dad did something, he didn't cut corners. He

constructed us a sandbox that looked more like a clubhouse as it had a roof and benches too. This was my brother's favorite.

Dad fabricated a three-foot-deep in-ground swimming pool from a grain bin that he had acquired from the factory where he worked. This was my sister's favorite.

Dad brought home a tractor seat, welded it on a metal drain pipe that was six feet in diameter, laid it on its side, burying the lower fourth and voilà...we had a tunnel-train. All the kids on the block could sit on top and straddle the train engine. We could rock side to side in unison to get it wobbling fast.

Dad stenciled our names and birthdates on it for colorful decorations. What fun. And it served a practical purpose as he wanted to remember our birthdays and make us feel treasured.

Of course, we had a swing set, too. But it was no ordinary swing set. It was an industrial strength set with trapeze bars. Where my father found these things, I'll never know.

He not only specialized in big toys, he made small ones too. Take our stilts, for instance. They were great entertainment. Or the unicycle he welded together from old bicycle parts then painted shiny red. This was Kathy's least favorite as she fell from it breaking her tailbone.

You name it; we had it. Although the parts for the toys didn't cost much, there was a price to pay. Most obviously, my Dad invested his time designing and building them.

An even larger time commitment was required of my mother. Since every kid on the block thought our yard was the best ever, she acquired some additional jobs like babysitter, paramedic, water waitress, and snack server.

~

MY DAD AND MOM USED THEIR TIME, TALENTS AND TREASURES TO serve God and their family. We were never lacking even though we never once had a new car, always had two renters that lived on our property and commonly shopped at garage sales. (I still enjoy shopping second hand as I found the dress I am wearing on the cover of this book for $7.99 at Goodwill.)

My father was hardworking and while he never had a college education he put all of us and my mother through college. I have even more respect for my parents as I look back and have a better understanding of their money management.

Perhaps that is why I choose to find **wonder** today in an unlikely place when I opened my Bible to *The Parable of the Three Servants*. In *Matthew 25:14-29 Jesus explains the Kingdom of Heaven by telling the story of a man who was going on a long trip.

So, he called together his employees. Dividing his money in proportion to their abilities, he gave five bags of silver to one, two bags of silver to another, and one bag of silver to the last. Then he left.

As you may remember, the employee who received the five bags of silver worked hard to earned five more.

The employee with two bags of silver also went to work and doubled the money.

But the employee who received the one bag of silver buried it in a hole. Then he did nothing at all every day for days on end.

After a long time, their employer returned calling them to give an account of how they had used his money.

The employee whom had been entrusted with five bags of silver came forward with five more.

His boss was very pleased and praised him saying:

"'Well done. You are an excellent, trustworthy worker. Because
you have been faithful in handling your responsibilities,
I will give you more.
Let's celebrate.
Treats on me.'"

Similarly, the servant who had received the two bags of silver earned two more. Again, his boss was pleased praising him exactly as he had praised the first servant. Then the servant with the one bag of silver came and said:

"'Boss, I knew you had high expectations of me,
but I was afraid I would lose your money,
so I buried it.'"

I find this incredibly sad. If we take the excuse as truth, the worker says he was fearful of loosing. While I certainly understand and have experienced fear, the worker *feared* his boss because he didn't *know* his boss.

His boss was fair, like my dad.

His boss had common sense, like my dad.

His boss expected the best from him, like my dad.

His boss wanted him to succeed, like my dad wanted me to succeed. Next we learn that his boss was justifiably angry asking why he didn't at least use common sense and deposit it in the bank to gain interest. Then the boss took the one bag of silver and gave it to the employee who had shown the most diligence saying:

> "'To those who use well what they are given,
> even more will be given,
> and they will have an abundance.
> But from those who do nothing,
> even what little they have will be taken away.'"

In some translations of the parable, bags of gold are given rather than silver. In the King James Bible "talents" are given. A "talent" was the largest unit of Jewish measure (Exodus 38:25). This is significant.

While the exact dollar value in today's economy is not important, Jesus wants us to know that in this parable he was entrusting his servants with huge amounts of his vast wealth.

What is also noteworthy is that the wealthy employer–Who represents God–gave to each of his employees based on their talents. He didn't overwhelm them with expectations that were beyond their skill set or intellectual capacity.

Which brings me back to my dad–who had a high school education–but would readily admit that he had more "street smarts" or common sense than he had "book smarts." He wanted his children to have both, being balanced.

My dad worked at Blaw Knox, a factory that made farm equipment until he was nearly forty, then he was employed by the Mattoon Street Department. He picked up trash, cleared snow, laid concrete and repaired most anything, leading crews of men.

He was known for being hard-working and fair, never expecting more from his fellow workers than their ability. He led by example. But he also never had much of a stomach for those who were outright lazy, those who didn't pull their fair share, leaving the load for others to carry.

I still remember seeing him sad when he knew we had not done our best shaking his head in disappointment. If we offered an explanation for our laziness he would listen and say:

"Excuses are a waste of words."

Then when we were little he would kneel down so that he could look us straight in the eye when he reminded us:

"Don't waste your words."

Dad spent his words wisely building us up encouraging us to try new things. I still remember how he would complement me when I completed a job well.

I had a flair for cleaning things up to make them look new, for decorating and for organizing. He would stand back and admire my work and nod his head in loving approval saying:

"Sweetheart, you can sure make 'somethin' out of 'nothin'!"

To this day, one of my greatest pleasures is to find something that is imperfect and to restore it. I learned this from my earthly Father. I have also learned that my Heavenly Father is the Master at perfecting and restoring.

Our Father created us, so He knows what talents He has given us. He knows our gifts. He wants us to accept His gifts then use and multiply them, so that we have an abundance to share.

This brings us back to the story Jesus told about His Father in *The Parable of the Three Servants*. In my New Living Translation Bible, it is entitled *The Parable of Loaned Money*. Having *loaned* each servant gifts *according to their talents,* He expected that they used their time wisely to multiply their gifts.

The boss in the parable shares a lot in common with my dad. They both thought excuses were a *waste of words* and laziness was a *waste of talents*. My father never rewarded laziness and neither does our Heavenly Father. He wants better for us.

THE JOURNEY FORWARD:

Today when I think of talents, I don't think of a unit of measure, rather I think of aptitudes or skills. While you may not have five bags of silver or gold, you do have unique talents, aptitudes and skills.

Can you cook?

Bake?

Organize?

Lead?

Sing?

You get the idea. What you may think is *ordinary* can become *extra-ordinary* and multiplied in His hands. Whatever you and I do have, we can use for His glory. Like my dad did when he made our cool teeter totter, can you vow to bless those "up and down and around" you on your journey forward?

CAR WASHES AND BLOW DRYERS

*W*hat do both car washes and blow dryers have in common? For me, both are **wonders** that delight my children. My three-year-old's favorite outing this month is to go to the car wash. She hides her eyes in excitement as the car is automatically pulled forward into the building. Sitting on my lap behind the steering wheel, her giggles boomerang off the windows as they are bombarded with water.

"I'm not ascared," she bounces and announces in exhilaration molding the word–afraid and scared–into one new word as the intensity of the noise from the water escalates. She is **wowed** by the whole process.

My son is equally blown away with **wonder** by the blow dryer. He watches intensely as I dry my hair. As he bounces in his Johnny Jump-Up®, his eyes are glued first to me, and then to my hair that is waving wildly, then to the dryer itself. He loves to feel the warm air fly past his face. I oblige. And he jumps toward the sky, thrilled and giggling in astonishment. What small **wonders** amaze children.

I MARVEL AT MY CHILDREN'S ABILITY TO FIND **WONDER** IN unremarkable places. And I am reminded of one of my favorite of King David's songs.

The nine verses of *Psalm 8 leaves blow dryers and car washes in the dust. There we are told that God's glory is magnified by His majestic works, so much so that toddlers take notice:

> Nursing **infants gurgle** choruses about you...
> I look up at your macro-skies, dark and enormous,
> your handmade sky-jewelry,
> moon and stars mounted in their settings.
> Then I look at my micro-self and **wonder.**

Maybe I have always liked this passage because it points us to the **wonders** of God in the heavens comparing them to handmade jewelry. I've dabbled making jewelry. Mine is pretty basic and never turns out as good as I imagined it in my mind. But God's jeweled skies are beyond what I can even fathom.

The heavens make King David feel unimportant yet in reading the remainder of the Psalm, we can see that he knows that God doesn't thinks that we are insignificant:

"What are mere mortals that you should think about them,
human beings that you should care for them?
Yet you made them only a little lower than God
and crowned them with glory and honor.
You gave them charge of everything you made,
putting all things under their authority..."

Did you notice where we rank in God's Hierarchy? We are important to God. I find it amazing that He crowned us with glory and put us in charge of His creation. We are most fulfilled when we return to Him the honor we receive by striving to live a holy life (Matt. 5:6).

THE JOURNEY FORWARD:

While simple activities like driving through a car wash or drying your hair may not seem **wonder** worthy, a sunrise or sunset is a worthy **W.O.W.** moment God provides every day.

How long has it been since you have paused to watch how beautifully He ushers in the morning and how magnificently He brings your day's journey to a close? Could you take time today to relax and enjoy His majestic show.

THE CRISPER DRAWER

oday I made an exciting discovery. The crisper drawer in my refrigerator has a high and a low setting. I learned it is to regulate humidity. Apparently low humidity keeps fruits drier, reducing premature rotting. High humidity is best for green leafy vegetables that will wilt with less moisture.

Since the day we moved into our home and adopted the existing refrigerator, our crisper's humidity setting has been parked indecisively right in the middle. To be perfectly honest, before today, I thought a crisper drawer was a psychological ploy by manufacturers to make us think that these deep drawers really keep vegetables crisper.

I don't know about your crisper drawer, but mine should more appropriately be called a rotter drawer. I only occasionally open it for fear of what I will find. When I do muster up the gumption, it's usually only long enough to shove in some new, unsuspecting vegetables that I bought at the store. Little did they know with whom they would share their new home.

My drawer houses green onions that are wilted beyond recognition. Cucumbers that have become limp and slimy with age. Carrots that have shriveled and hardened.

Bananas that are bruised and black...but not so bruised they need to be thrown away. You know the kind. They aren't appealing enough to eat, but you want to keep them from drawing gnats, so you toss them in the drawer until they become mush, oozing all over the bottom.

The problem with crispers is that you can just shut the drawer, so you don't have to look at the healthy foods each time you open your refrigerator. Then you don't have to feel a tinge of remorse when you grab for the jar of ice-cream topping.

Yes indeed, my rotter drawer is a necessity...where else could I make penicillin from oranges?

SOME OF US HAVE THE SPIRITUAL EQUIVALENT TO ROTTER DRAWERS in our lives. Do let me explain. We have little rotten sins we tuck away in a drawer where few can see. Of course, those folks at church would never suspect us of having a loose tongue. You know the type...when you're mad, rotten little words ooze out when you're squeezed like a rotten tomato.

Some folks hide apples of anger in their drawers. Others

hide grapes of gossip. Still others have their drawers filled with pears of pride. Some have humongous grapefruits of greed.

Many have a few stray radishes of resentment that have rolled to the back to rot. Squashed tomatoes of temperance are common as are putrefied potatoes of pessimism. Celery of self-ishness and lemons of lust battle for room with the broccoli of backsliding.

Might we need to clean the rotten fruits of the flesh out of our crisper drawers and ask the Holy Spirit to replace them with wholesome spiritual fruit? Galatians 5:22 is a staple in Scripture for me. Here we are given a shopping list of the fruit of the Spirit:

> "But the Holy Spirit produces this kind of fruit in our lives:
> love, joy, peace, patience, kindness, goodness,
> faithfulness, gentleness, and self-control.
> There is no law against these things."

I ask myself: Do I have the fruit of faithfulness in my work life? Am I gentle with a person who cuts me off in traffic? Am I patient with my children and my spouse?

If you're anything like me, I find my crisper drawer needs cleaned often. It seems that every time I turn around, I am finding something rotten that needs to be thrown away. The natural course for fruit that lies unused is to rot. God wants us to enjoy and use our fruits. We can share our fruits and bless others bringing God glory.

As Christians we are filled with the fruit of the Spirit. Each of us has a full crisper drawer; none of them are empty. It is a miracle performed by the Holy Spirit Himself.

As we use our fruit of the Spirit, the drawer is replenished. The fruit never runs out...but sin can creep in. And the result of sin is a rotten mess. Take it from Adam and Eve. After they ate of the forbidden fruit, their lives of perfection turned putrid.

THE JOURNEY FORWARD:

Might you have the strength and time today to clean out your refrigerator's crisper drawer while reflecting on God's promise below? I would much rather have "all spiritual blessings in heavenly places" described in Ephesians 1:3 than the rotten fruit in my drawer.

"Blessed be the God and Father of our Lord Jesus Christ,
who hath blessed us with all spiritual blessings
in heavenly places in Christ."

ENTERTAINING ANGELS

y grandmother, Mary Nale, lived to be 94 years old, which gave her lots of time to tell the stories she most treasured from motherhood. She and Grandpa, who lived to be 103, raised two boys during the depression.

My grandfather worked on the railroad. They, like many other families, had few luxuries and lived in a one-bedroom brown home on a small half lot separated by an alley from the railroad tracks. When times became exceedingly tight, they rented the front rooms of their house out to a second family, which forced them to share their kitchen and sleep in the cold, unfinished basement.

Rarely did my grandmother entertain, but one morning was different. In preparation for her lady guests she had cinnamon rolls that were covered with white confection icing tucked away in a secluded bottom cabinet. Little did she know my father—who was young enough to act innocent but old enough to know better—had discovered her hiding place.

While she was chatting with the women, downstairs little Clifford was busy bending the rule. He knew he was *not to eat* the rolls, so he didn't. Grandma explained that he very carefully "licked them plum clean" leaving them perfectly positioned on the plate. And she added "Why, they were so clean, they glistened."

She explained that had you not known they were once iced, you never would have guessed. But let the record show that my father hadn't laid a finger on the rolls. Only his little tongue licked across the line clearly laid down by Grandma. So there she stood with a batch of beautiful, bare rolls and her guests, who expected something with their tea.

Though I heard the story hundreds of times, it is only now as I am sitting at my computer decades later that I realize she never told us what she said and served. Oh, how I wish I could ask her. Knowing Grandma, she didn't focus on the frustration but rather my dad's sticky little grin.

As we hunger for wonder, I fondly remember my Grandma and this story. She went to heaven one year ago today. In her memory, I baked cinnamon rolls for my family this morning. Alyssa nearly exploded with excitement when I showed her how to pop open the cardboard refrigerator roll!

ENTERTAINING ANGELS | 169

My two little ones also seem to like the icing best. Their sticky, sweet kisses leave remnants of frosting on my cheek and I have to smile back as their darling faces light up with the **wonder** of a special treat. I now better understand why my Grandma treasured this story.

After scrubbing their sticky fingers and faces, I am left to reflect on my Grandma's entertaining. It brings Hebrews 13:2 to mind where Paul also speaks of entertaining. He tells us to:

> "Keep on loving each other as brothers and sisters.
> Don't forget to show hospitality to strangers,
> for some who have done this
> have entertained angels without realizing it!"

This makes me **wonder** if I have ever entertained angels without realizing it? Maybe we have not had any in our homes for rolls, but have we encountered angels perhaps at the grocery store?

Or maybe at the post office?

Or at the doctor's office?

We often think of angels having wings and glowing, but we know from encounters with angels in the Bible, that they can look just like you and me (Genesis 18). Sometimes they are sent to defend us (Matthew 18:10) or help minister to us (Daniel 10:13). Other times—like in the passage above from Hebrews—we are told to show hospitality and minister to them.

Which makes me also **wonder**, do I have a heart of hospitality toward strangers? I want to. Like you, I see people every week who are in need, mostly holding a sign that asks for help. Honestly, it makes me a bit uncomfortable. How does it make you feel?

My husband and I have very different responses. Perhaps you do too. You may also have questions, like my husband. What decisions or circumstances have brought a person to the place where they are desperate enough to beg? Even the verb "beg" makes me uncomfortable to type.

While I certainly don't know the answer, I do know the scene that Jesus describes in The Final Judgement in *Matthew 25:35-36 and just the thought of it, makes us reevaluate how we live.

We are told that Jesus will arrive in blazing beauty with all His angels and He will take His place on a glorious throne. All the people who have ever been born will be arranged before Him and He will sort them out like a shepherd sorts out sheep and goats. The sheep will go to His right and the goats to His left. Jesus–our King–will welcome those on His right saying:

"I was hungry and you fed me,
I was thirsty and you gave me a drink,
I was homeless and you gave me a room,
I was shivering and you gave me clothes,
I was sick and you stopped to visit,
I was in prison and you came to me."

As we **hunger for wonder**, are we looking for others who hunger? I could look harder. Honestly, I trust Jesus and know that He will bless me when I bless others. Which leads me to ask, could God satiate my **hunger for wonder** by reaching out to those who also hunger…or thirst? Those who are homeless and need weather appropriate clothing? Those who are sick and lonely? Those who are imprisoned?

What image comes to mind when you think of people who have needs like these? In our journey to see the *extra*ordinary in the ordinary, could we also begin to see the extra-ordinary need in ordinary people?

People like us, who also thirst and **hunger for the wonder** of knowing Christ and feeling fulfilled by our Creator? People who are sick with sadness but may look perfectly healthy on the outside? People who long for a place where they can feel loved and at home even though they are not physically houseless? People who are imprisoned by pain from the past but may look free as they drive their cars on the freeways just like we do?

There is *extraordinary* need all around us in *ordinary* people… people who look just like you and me. Perhaps you are in need today.

We each have days of need. Saint Paul certainly did. We can read about a season in his life in 2 Timothy 4:10-15 where he shares that three of his dearest friends had deserted him and only Luke still came around.

Like us, Saint Paul felt lonely. He asked for some basic necessities like his coat. And he wanted his books to read. I am so grateful that this extra-ordinary man shared his ordinary needs. What needs do you have today?

THE JOURNEY FORWARD:

In honor of my Grandma Nale, I made *ordinary* rolls from a cardboard roll I bought in the *ordinary* dairy section of an *ordinary* supermarket. What can you do that is *ordinary* but may seem *extraordinary*, even angelic, to someone?

SHINING PENNIES

A SHINING EXAMPLE

*T*hough I don't remember her first name, I do clearly remember her smiling face. I remember her kind eyes and I remember her gentle touch.

She was the pleasantly plump grandma who wore heavy stockings with orthopedic shoes and hobbled down the church basement stairs to sit behind the card table. She collected our lunch money every day when I went to St. Mary's Grade School.

She was a resilient volunteer who offered more than just her time. She gave her own money. If you forgot your two quarters for lunch, she always had a few spare ones she could find in the pocket of her frock as she winked at you.

Oh, she would write your name in her spiral note book and the amount you owed, but you knew it was merely a formality required by the lunchroom staff. Record keeping was not her higher calling.

174 | WINDOWS OF WONDER

As I think back, I have to laugh. As a child, I truly thought she was there to collect shiny new pennies. That's what she always told us. Her face would light up when we dumped pennies on her table.

As she would count them out she would tell us of her plans to give all the shiny ones to her grandson so that he could fly to Florida someday. As an adult, I realize that this generous grandma shuffled down to her metal folding chair for more than just shiny pennies.

She was called.

She had a greater purpose.

She was warm and reassuring.

She was a comforter for kids who were cold and hungry.

Though her hands were distorted from arthritis and colored with brown spots and blue bruises, her touch across the table was soothing.

She cared.

She listened to us.

She asked about our day.

Just her abiding presence made us feel better. Suddenly it no longer mattered that vacuum had only one "c" and two "u's" rather than two "c's" and one "u." It didn't matter if you kicked the ball out of bounds at recess....TWICE. And it didn't matter if no one bought your healthy oatmeal raisin cookies at the bake sale that your mother insisted would sell "like hotcakes."

She had a way of erasing the bad, just like she erased our names in the spiral notebook when she paid the debt we owed for hot lunches. Why so many years later would I remember her embodiment of grace? Because her service made a lasting impression on one shy little girl named Lisa. So today as we come near the end of our journey, let's reflect on her shining example near the end of her earthly journey. Today her service is our source of **wonder.**

As I HUNGER FOR WONDER, I THINK ABOUT THE LUNCH LADY AND ask myself, what impression will I leave by my service? For what do I strive? Unfortunately, sometimes you and I strive for pennies....hundreds of thousands of millions of pennies.

If you and your spouse earn $100,000 a year, you toil for 1,000 million pennies. It seems senseless to measure our worth by copper disks with heads and tails. Doesn't it?

The world cannot make heads or tails out of how God measures worth. His system for service is outlined by none other than Saint Matthew–a man who specialized in collecting coins for taxation before his conversion. He had learned the lesson of shiny pennies and servanthood only too well and outlines it simply in *Matthew 23:11-12:

"Do you want to stand out?
Then step down.
Be a servant.
If you puff yourself up, you'll get the wind knocked out of you.
But if you're content to simply be yourself,
your life will count for plenty."

Don't you wish that all tax collectors would be as straight forward and easy to understand as Saint Matthew? Now for the harder question, do you and I really believe this?

If we truly believe that the greatest person is the one who serves, why don't you and I make it our life goal to serve others? Those who continually seek ways to serve others have a humble spirit. They also seem to have a happiness that transcends explanation. They have a contentment that defies worldly understanding.

Those who strive to serve others as if they were serving the Lord incarnate have a perspective that is radically different from those who labor in frustration, thinking that their hard work goes unnoticed.

Imagine the difference in our attitude if we worked truly believing that it was a task to which we had been commissioned by the Almighty God. What a difference Mark 10:31 would make on our perspective of daily chores if we truly understood that:

> "Many that are first shall be last;
> and the last first."

Imagine a housewife in stretched-out sweats wearing yellow rubber gloves with her hair pulled up in a ponytail being seated in a position of more prestige than a CEO dressed in a suit from Sachs with a Windows® watch on her wrist.

Imagine yourself receiving more attention and accolades than your favorite movie star. Someday it may be reality. If you find yourself longing to be noticed and appreciated, please don't lose heart. And above all don't grow weary and depressed. Your day may be just around the celestial corner.

Heaven will be more extravagant than Hollywood's Oscars and the awards will be more lasting than a gold-plated statue of a bald man for your mantle. Though few here may recognize your humble service, rest assured Christ Himself will. Until that day, however, Saint Paul has given us some solid gold advice in ** 1 Thessalonians 4:11:

> "Study to be quiet,
> and to do your own business,
> and to work with your own hands."

Notice the verb "study." It comes from the Greek word–philotimeomai–which means "to be ambitious" or "to strive eagerly." Here we have three goals in life for which we are to strive ambitiously: we are to be quiet, to mind our own affairs and to work.

The New Living Translation Bible says it this way:

> "Make it your goal to live a quiet life,
> minding your own business and
> working with your hands…
> Then people who are not believers
> will respect the way you live."

Sometimes I make life so much more complex than it needs

to be. With warm memories I chuckle when I think about the affectionate grandma who collected my lunch money. She wasn't distracted by pennies from her higher calling.

Though the hot lunches nourished me for an afternoon of studies, her example of love, generosity and kindness has nourished my soul for many seasons. I **wonder** if her grandson ever made it to Florida on the shiny pennies she collected, and I **wonder** if he ever thanked her for her enduring gift of grace? And...I **wonder** if her name was Grace?

THE JOURNEY FORWARD:

Can you look for the shiniest penny you can find in your wallet and put it next to your kitchen sink this week? Each time you see it, be inspired to serve others.

THE GIVING TREE

*A*s we near the end of our journey together, I want you
to know how much I have enjoyed walking with you,
peeking through God's **Windows of Wonder.**

But before we say goodbye and you close this book, I want to
share my favorite childhood book with you. Written in 1963
Shel Silverstein wrote *The Giving Tree* which is now a children's
classic.

It is the story of a giving apple tree and a boy through all
stages of life. As a child, the boy loves climbing the tree's trunk,
swinging from her branches and eating her apples.

But as he grew, he has less time for the tree and visits her
only when he wants things. Desiring to make the boy happy at
each of these stages, the tree gives parts of herself for him to use.
She gives…

her apples to gain him money...

her branches to build him a home...

her trunk to make a him a boat.

When the boy returns as an old man, the tree is a stump with nothing left to give. Only then the boy realizes that the tree has all he really wants and needs. *The Giving Tree* stump provides a quiet place to sit and rest. Together again, they both are happy.

BEFORE NAP TIME TODAY AS I READ THIS BOOK TO MY DAUGHTER, I was sad. Both sad that someday she will grow up and sad that our journey in search of **wonder** is coming to a close.

This story reminds me of the lunch lady from yesterday as well as the *Parable of the Loving Father*, which is the title I much prefer over the more common title of *The Parable of the Prodigal Son*. Have you ever noticed the similarities between the characters in this parable and *The Giving Tree*?

Jesus tells us that there was once a man who had two sons. The younger demanded his inheritance early. So the Father obliged dividing the property. Before long the younger son headed off into the sunset looking for adventure. He lived a loose life squandering his Dad's hard-earned money (Luke 15:11-14).

What the text doesn't tell us is what those who heard this parable innately understood based on their Hebrew culture. In asking for his inheritance early, the son was symbolically saying that his father was dead to him, severing the already troubled relationship.

Then Jesus tells us that a famine struck, and the son took a job feeding pigs, which was ironic because pigs were considered unclean and forbidden as food for any Jew. The boy was starving for even the pig slop.

Then one day he had a **W.O.W.** moment and remembered how well fed his father's servants were, deciding he would rather serve his dad than starve to death.

His Father's heart ached.

He missed his son and remembered when he was young, before rebellion rocked their world. Now he woke up each morning hoping this might be the day his boy would return. As the weeks rolled into months and years, he never stopped looking for his return.

Then one evening, he saw a silhouette on the horizon…

Could it be…

dare he hope it be…

his boy?

The figure looked thinner and more haggard. He walked hesitantly, lacking confidence. His shoulders sagged. The cocky swagger was missing...but, yes, the figure was his son.

Bedraggled. But walking toward him. Still too far to see the expression on his face, the father leaned down to grab the bottom of his robe, hiking it up so that he could sprint with full strides toward his child.

He didn't care what others might think about a man of his

stature running with his robe pulled up. He didn't even care what his family thought. His only thought was that his son was lost and now he is found.

Home.

Home at last.

His heart pounded in excitement. Tears came to his eyes. He kissed his son's cheeks and the top of his head. He didn't care that his boy smelled like bovine.

They embraced. Then his son pulled away and began a speech as he looked at his mud encrusted feet. He explained that he had sinned against both God and his Dad and that he didn't deserve to be called his son (Luke 15:21).

But the father didn't need to hear his son's apology. He saw contrition in his child's eyes. He felt his tears when he kissed his cheeks. His Dad knew by his stench that mistakes had been made.

But today was not a day to remember regrets. It was a day to rejoice! His Dad commanded that he be given a robe fit for a royal prince. Along with it, he was given the family signature ring that showed he had full access to sign his Father's name to any legal document.

His dad had the servants go out to the pasture to bring in the holiday heifer. This was going to be a feast to remember. It would be a day he never forgot—the day his child came home.

Jesus was such a wonderful storyteller, and this is one of my favorites because it speaks of wonderful beginnings—not endings. It is a story of restoration. A story of renewal that leads to an *extra-ordinary* party on what could have otherwise been an *ordinary*, even depressing day.

Every day in our journey we too have come home to our Father, the very Source of our **wonder.** Every day He has given us something *extra-ordinary* in the *ordinary.*

Like the father in the story who surveyed the horizon and soared the moment he saw his son's silhouette, God watches and waits for us. Like the father in the story, He knows our silhouette and doesn't care where we have wandered or what we have done, He is just glad we are finally home.

Like the boy in *The Giving Tree* or *The Parable of the Loving Father,* you may have wandered away, grown up, grown busy or grown distant, but always know that **wonder** awaits you at home. Whether you are a prodigy (a marvel or wonder) or a prodigal (wastefully extravagant) or someone in between (like me), you are your Father's child and He wants you to **come home when you hunger.** You might think you are *ordinary,* but He thinks you are *extraordinary!*

THE JOURNEY FORWARD

I wish we all lived in the same city, so we could meet for coffee and chat sharing how we have experienced His **wonder.** Someday in heaven, let's set aside some time for that. But for today, I do have a fun idea based on the parable we just read about *The Loving Father.*

Did you notice that he gave his son a ring when he returned? Do you have a wonderful ring that you don't ordinarily wear;

one that you slip on for the remainder of the month to remind you to go to your Father when you **hunger for His wonder?**

The ring doesn't have to be expensive to remind you to look for Him in **W.O.W.** moments daily. Perhaps if you don't have one, you would like to buy yourself one in His remembrance?

I DON'T DO WINDOWS

We've almost completed our **Windows of Wonder** journey and I have a question for you...Do you "do windows?"

My daughter loves to clean windows, or maybe I should more correctly share, she loves to spray Windex®. It doesn't even matter if it is solution in the bottle or water. She's not picky. She just loves to squirt the spray bottle. She totally douses every square inch of the window, though she applies very little elbow grease with the paper towels.

My one-year-old son, on the other hand, loves to play with the paper towels. He begins by taking the roll and throwing it around the room until every inch has been removed. Then he seems to enjoy seeing just how many pieces he can tear it into...which means that I no longer have only the windows to clean.

It's not that I mind doing windows, because in truth, I rather enjoy it. I smile seeing the sun shine through without a streak in sight. And I enjoy seeing the absence of little Dum Dum® sucker smudges, though I know that someday I will long for prints on the storm door glass.

SO, WE'VE COME FULL CIRCLE. WE STARTED WITH THE STORM door my little brother somersaulted through as a kid when my dad removed the Plexiglas and now we are ending at my sticky storm door.

This leads me to ponder the question...As Christians could we be called to "do windows?" To clean off whatever clouds us from seeing God's **wonder** and grace in our lives, then sharing that grace?

Based on hundreds of Scriptures in the New Testament alone, I believe that God calls each of us. Though we are not all called to be pastors *in* a church, He does call each of us to be ministers of love *to* the church and to those *outside* the churches.

Sounds like a pretty big task, but our God is a pretty big God and He's very willing to help in any way possible whenever we ask. Is there anything that clouds or dirties our spiritual windows so that you and I are less likely to see His **wonder** and grace?

While Jesus never shared a parable about cleaning windows, He did share a parable about planting seeds that focuses on the condition of people's hearts. It's another of my favorite parables because He talks about farming, which also takes me full circle back to my roots in the farming community of Mattoon.

Jesus compares people to seeds that fall on different types of soil when the farmer scatters seed by taking God's Word to others in Mark 4:14-20.

The seed that fell on the beaten down path represents those who hear about Christ who died for their sins, only to have Satan like a bird, pluck it away.

The seed on the rocky soil represents those who hear the Christian message and seem to be growing joyfully. But they lack roots and they don't last long. When drought hits and life hurts, they wilt (just like my last name).

The seed that fell in with the weeds represents others who hear God's Word also, but weedy worries and want for wealth crowd it out so that no fruit is produced.

The seed that fell on rich soil represents those who truly hear and hold onto God's word. They produce a harvest of thirty, sixty, or even a hundred times as much as had been planted.

So in the four paragraphs above, Jesus outlines four types of people based on the condition of their soil or heart: hardened soil, rocky soil, weedy soil and good soil. Which makes me ask myself what kind of heart do I have?

I want a life like the rich, fertile soil in Mattoon, that is as dark and as soft as potting soil thanks to glaziers that scrapped a gold mine of top soil straight to the fields of central Illinois. Growing up, I never thought our soil was special. Then I moved to Kansas City with flat fields of hard clay. It does produce wheat, but not without the farmer's fight.

What type of soil have you experienced in your life? Oh, how I want to produce an abundant harvest, so that I am a blessing to those who **hunger for wonder** and need grace in their lives. I need God's Word to grow in my heart so that I have a harvest that is thirty, sixty and one hundred-fold to share with my family and friends. Do you need a harvest of **wonder** and grace?

People are looking for the extraordinary in the ordinary. They crave miracles in the mundane and it all starts with grace. We were extended loving grace through God's Son. Though our occupations will vary, we each are called.

We don't have to be missionaries in Africa like my friend Cyndi to impact the world. We don't have to be a physician like my husband to help those who need to be healed. We can be a manager or a designer, a mom or a dad.

God can use our *ordinary* talents for an *extra-ordinary* purpose. Can you see what God would want you to accomplish today or are the windows of your reality smeared with the handprints of the world? I need to daily clean the window of *my* will off, so I can see *His* will. *1 Corinthians 1:9 provides a scriptural squirt of Windex:

"God, who got you started in this spiritual adventure,
shares with us the life of his Son and our Master Jesus.
He will never give up on you.
Never forget that."
And that, my dear friends, is the greatest **wonder** of all!

THE JOURNEY FORWARD:

You and I together are called to "do windows" cleaning off whatever clouds us from seeing God through His **Window of Wonder.** He tells us in Ephesians 2:10 that we are His "masterpieces" who He perfected through His Son so that we can do the good things that He planned for us!

On your journey forward today–and everyday–will you look for those "good things," those **W.O.W.** things, He planned for you each day?

MY JOURNEY FORWARD

AFTERWARD

*N*early twenty years ago, I had a **W.O.W.** moment as I stood at my kitchen sink witnessing a doe and her two bouncing baby fawns. Since then, I've washed a lot of dishes and a lot of windows.

Funny thing about dishes, windows and life, none stay spotless for long. By nature, I'm a Type A perfectionist. By grace, I'm a child of God who is still learning to savor perfect **W.O.W.** moments in my imperfect life.

I still **hunger for wonder**!

But when I crave for more than the mundane, I know where to look. I look to my Creator, Who never ceases to **W.O.W.** me. Through the years, He has directed my path and those of my children.

When my daughter was a preschooler, one morning I woke up to her holding an empty bottle that had held her pink bubble gum flavored Amoxicillin. She confidently bounced and announced,

"I drank it *all-l-l-l* gone, so I will get *all-l-l-l* better."

Back then, I **wondered** what she would become when she grew up. Now I know. Alyssa is a beautiful pharmacist who serves the Lord dispensing both encouragement and medicine. She loves God and her hubby–a Marine named Robert.

While Alyssa chose to follow in my footsteps as a pharmacist, my son is following in my husband's as he studies to become a physician. And my little brother, Barney Blue Bell, who wanted to be a "pop man" when he got big, is now an executive for a beverage company. His colleagues know him as Brian Nale.

Indeed, life has a way of coming full circle. I still remember what my undergraduate English professor, Dr. Dixon, shared with me at the end of the semester before I left for pharmacy school. He told me that I was his "biggest failure" explaining that he had failed to convince me I should become a writer, not a pharmacist.

I don't know where Dr. Dixon is today, but if he's reading this, I hope he smiles. He knew I loved adjectives, alliteration, and imagery always returning my papers with lots of red ink in an effort to teach restraint. This makes me wonder what he would think of this book.

Now Dave and I are contemplating our next chapter. While I'm not sure what this will bring, I am sure **W.O.W.** moments will never grow old. And someday, I'll arrive and a window won't separate me from the **wonder** that my heavenly Father has planned for all of eternity.

It's been an honor to share this journey forward with you, together as we **hunger for wonder.**

I would love to hear about your **W.O.W.** moments.

You can share them with me and others on
facebook.com/RxForTheSoulfulHeart or
RxForTheSoulfulHeart.com

CONTACT LISA TO SPEAK

AT AN EVENT

*If you would like Lisa to speak at your church
or upcoming event,
contact her at
RxForTheSoulfulHeart.com*

~

Lisa Wilt is an emerging author and inspirational speaker who has a love for learning creatively. She has been a contributing author for two books. By faith, she has written multiple Women's Bible Studies and led numerous Women's Retreats. Creating Sunday School Curriculum, Lisa has taught for over three decades. She continues to lead Christ's Hospitality Ministry at her local church.

By profession, Lisa is an award-winning pharmacist who has worked since 1988 in community pharmacy and the pharmaceutical industry.

By grace, Lisa and her husband–a physician–have two children who have followed in their footpath: Alyssa is a pharmacist dispensing both medicine and encouragement while Garrett is an honored medical student.

As her family will tell you, Lisa's weaknesses are thrift-store bargains and chocolate chips.

facebook.com/RxForTheSoulfulHeart

instagram.com/rxforthesoulfulheart

twitter.com/RxSoulfulHeart

Made in the USA
Lexington, KY
12 September 2018